Agricultural Activity in Poland: A Fiscal and Legal Study

Lex et Res Publica
Polish Legal and Political Studies
Edited by Anna Jaroń

Volume 15

Marcin Burzec / Beata Kucia-Guściora / Paweł Smoleń

Agricultural Activity in Poland: A Fiscal and Legal Study

PETER LANG

Bibliographic Information published by the Deutsche Nationalbibliothek
The Deutsche Nationalbibliothek lists this publication
in the Deutsche Nationalbibliografie; detailed bibliographic
data is available online at http://dnb.d-nb.de.

Library of Congress Cataloging-in-Publication Data
A CIP catalog record for this book has been applied for at the
Library of Congress.

"Cover illustration: The Harvesters painted by Pieter Bruegel the Elder.
Credit Line: Rogers Fund, 1919"

The monograph comprises research conducted within a scientific project financed by Polish
National Science Centre. Number of project: 2013/09/B/HS5/04503.

This Publication was Reviewed by:
Prof. Soraya Rodríguez Losada (University of Vigo, Spain)
Prof. Patrycja Zawadzka (University of Wrocław, Poland)

ISSN 2191-3250
ISBN 978-3-631-81470-3 (Print)
E-ISBN 978-3-631-83467-1 (E-Book)
E-ISBN 978-3-631-83468-8 (EPUB)
E-ISBN 978-3-631-83469-5 (MOBI)
DOI 10.3726/b17557

Peter Lang – Berlin · Bern · Bruxelles · New York ·
Oxford · Warszawa · Wien

This publication has been peer reviewed.

www.peterlang.com

Table of Contents

Preface

In the era of economic globalization, individual states try to pursue effective agricultural support policies. There is a variety of instruments which can be used to influence agriculture. One of such instruments is an adequate tax policy design.

Undoubtedly, tax law solutions occupy an important place in the wide range of legal instruments that shape broadly understood agricultural activity. However, we should note that the concept of agricultural activity has no clear definition. Depending on the importance of agriculture to a given economy and other conditions (e.g. climatic, geographical, and infrastructural), various conceptions of taxation of such activity are used in practice. What appears crucial is the manner of taxing income from agricultural activity. Typically, this kind of activity remains subject to a specific form of income tax or land tax. This last concept is somewhat older and widely used, especially in socialist countries. Income tax, in turn, is prevalent in Western Europe. In certain countries, agricultural activity may enjoy partial or full tax exemption by virtue of agricultural development strategies.

In general, we notice a cautious approach to taxation of agricultural activity. Indeed, it manifests itself in the fact that any changes in the tax burden placed on this economic sector are intentionally lengthened: not only because of the specific nature of agricultural activity itself but also – and above all – for political reasons. We should also bear in mind that solutions applied to taxpayers occupied with agricultural activity should not lead to discriminatory policies against those who pursue non-agricultural economic activity. Another issue is the proper formulation of tax regulations for agricultural activity, so that they constitute a permanent element of an internally coherent tax system.

The issue of taxing agricultural activity in Poland has a particular social, economic, and even political importance. This is mostly for historical reasons. In recent years, agriculture has gone through too radical changes. Initially, these changes were part of the transition from a planned economy to a market economy. In the second stage, there began the process of integration of Polish agriculture into the common European policy. Thus, even a general overview of the problem allows us to assert that it comprises a wide range of different aspects which concurrently affect its complex matter. Undoubtedly, taxation of agricultural activity is one of the most controversial issues within tax law. Creating a sound tax system, which takes into consideration both the fiscal interest and the specific nature of agricultural production, is not an easy task. In this area, legal, economic, social, and political issues are strongly intertwined. All these factors contribute to the long-lasting, complicated character of the discussion on this subject. Many different, often mutually exclusive, conceptions emerge. The high political risk of such a reform is also of crucial importance.

In the current Polish conditions, the very need to reform agricultural taxation system falls beyond dispute. What remains controversial is the reform's direction, detailed provisions, and implementation schedule. Notwithstanding the choice of a specific conception of new taxation rules, we should stress the importance of adequate tax regulations for agricultural activity – regulations which may become part of a coherent tax system in Poland. To be sure, such a perspective exceeds the scope of this monograph, which deals primarily with issues related to agricultural and income taxes. Undoubtedly, however, it is these taxes that constitute the pillar of the fiscal burden placed on agricultural activity. Therefore, we consider it necessary to analyze the conditions – especially tax barriers – which exist in this area of Polish taxation policy. In this monograph, our intention is not only to present a theoretical and practical verification of the regulations currently applied in Poland but also to project the direction of reforms and outline an adequate model of taxing land and agricultural income in this country.

Chapter One: The Concept of Agricultural Activity in Tax Law

I. Principles of agricultural taxation: an overview

The design of each state's tax system hinges on its sovereignty, from which its tax jurisdiction derives. Thus, undoubtedly, the shape of tax regulations is influenced by the state's internal conditions, such as its budgetary needs, economic and social factors, but also its history. We cannot ignore the impact of economic globalization and the resulting international relations on the tax system, particularly as reflected in the process of tax harmonization under European Union law. These aspects are also evident in the design of the agricultural taxation system. Indeed, we can claim that each state's tax policy is bound to its own agricultural policy. This applies to the Polish tax policy (both now and in the past), which translates into a particular system of taxation of agriculture (agricultural activity). Namely, the taxation of agriculture and agricultural activity is not based a monotax system but rather constitutes a specific combination of certain taxes applicable in Poland, in whose structure one may distinguish agriculture-related elements from the so-called taxation standard. This distinction assumes a variety of forms. On the one hand, there is a separate agricultural tax with an unclear typology, while on the other hand, there is a distinction of special agricultural production branches, which fall under an income tax, from non-agricultural economic activities. The peculiar nature of the taxation of agricultural activity manifests itself also in the separation of agricultural taxation principles from the general tax system through an array of tax benefits designed exclusively for agricultural activity. In this context, the literature poses the question of whether the Polish system of taxation of agricultural activity is based on a uniform and coherent tax model, or rather is a set of taxation principles that do not conform to any known model.[1] Below, we shall present a general "roadmap" of Polish tax regulations which include an element related to agricultural activity or, more broadly, agriculture.

Within the doctrine of tax law, the discrimination between direct and indirect taxes is evident and unquestionable, as is the case with state and local

---

1 For more on this subject, see: M. Burzec, P. Smoleń, "Modele opodatkowania rolnictwa," in: *Opodatkowanie rolnictwa w Polsce. Weryfikacja założeń, perspektywa zmian*, ed. P. Smoleń (Warsaw, 2018), pp. 47–63.

government taxes. But one may find it more challenging to perform an unambiguous classification by nature of the tax if the criterion for this division is object-oriented and therefore entails a determination of the tax base. The doctrine of Polish tax law is not clear in this respect.[2] Therefore, we present a description of agricultural activity taxes without referring to the conventional approach to tax typology. Instead, we refer to object-oriented criteria and the comprehensiveness of legal coverage of a given form of agricultural activity.

The most significant agricultural activity tax currently in force in Poland is the **agricultural tax**.[3] It supplies the budgets of communes (gminas), but is not clear in terms of typology. Some describe the agricultural tax as a property tax, revenue tax, or revenue-property tax. However, it also has the features of a revenue-income tax, since, based on external factors, it taxes income from agricultural activity.[4] This tax defines the following concepts: agricultural activity and agricultural holding, land defined as agricultural land, and the categories of taxable persons, although they are not called "farmers" in the Law. A specific element of its structure is the tax base and tax rates, which bring it close to revenue tax. Namely, the tax base is a conversion hectare, unique to this type of tax, that accounts for the type, class, and location of agricultural land, with separate conversion rates for land below ponds. The tax rate varies, as it depends on the purchase price of a quintal of rye, that is, the average price charged in the previous tax year. There is a number of subjective and objective exemptions within the agricultural tax. The considerable range of these exemptions shows a significant privilege of the agricultural sector. They concern not only situations where land cannot be freely owned – for instance, land situated on a border road strip or excluded for water bodies – but also account for instances where land is used for agricultural activities and does not generate income (land under drainage or classified as underperforming). Some of these exemptions are clearly stimulative, aiming to expand or adapt land used for agricultural activities. Additional preferential elements of this tax include tax reliefs for natural disasters, agricultural holdings located on mountains or foothills, or investments. Another principle that we can

---

2 M. Kalinowski, "Rodzaje podatków i ich klasyfikacja oraz systemy podatkowe," in: *System prawa finansowego. Tom III. Prawo daninowe*, eds. L. Etel, J. Głuchowski, C. Kosikowski, E. Ruśkowski (Warsaw, 2010), pp. 67–88.

3 Act of November 15, 1984 on Agricultural Tax (Journal of Laws 2019, item 1256), hereinafter: Agricultural Tax Act.

4 For more on this subject, see: M. Burzec, "Podatek rolny," in: *Opodatkowanie rolnictwa w Polsce*. . ., p. 357; L. Etel, "Podatki przychodowo-dochodowo-majątkowe," in: *System prawa finansowego. Tom III. Prawo daninowe*. . ., from p. 305.

consider preferential, especially for natural persons, is the tax authority's determination of the tax amount. In conclusion, the amount of the agricultural tax largely depends on economic and natural conditions of exercising an agricultural activity, regardless of land type, use efficiency, or other important infrastructural factors.[5]

Under the provisions of the Polish agricultural tax, agricultural activity is excluded from **state income tax**: **personal income tax**[6] and **corporate income tax**.[7] Although agricultural activity is not subject to income taxes in Poland, the so-called special branches of agricultural production are. They are defined in both these taxes and taxed similarly to income from non-agricultural economic activity. The tax base is income, understood, in principle, as the positive difference between income and tax-deductible costs. At the same time, instead of actual income, natural persons can have their tax base determined with the legally defined standards for estimating annual income, which can constitute a tax preference. Such a possibility is not available to corporate income taxpayers, who are obliged to determine their actual income. In personal income tax, the taxpayers can benefit from preferential elements, such as tax reliefs, joint taxation of spouses, subjective exemptions, or preferential ways of determining advance tax payments. Similarly, in corporate income tax, in a manner that does not deviate from the standards, taxpayers who run special agricultural production branches can benefit from the capital group tax structure, tax reliefs, or tax exemptions, some of which are clearly agricultural in character.[8]

Natural persons that earn income indirectly related to conducting agricultural activity, among other things, from the sale of processed agricultural products, rural tourism services, and other agriculture-related services can take advantage of tax exemptions and, in some cases, simplified forms of taxation, such as a flat rate on registered income or a tax card.[9]

Apart from the two discussed, somewhat complementary categories of taxable objects – agricultural activity and special agricultural activity branches that

---

5 We will discuss the agricultural tax more broadly in Chapter Four.

6 Act of July 26, 1991 on Personal Income Tax (Journal of Laws 2019, item 1387 as amended), hereinafter: PIT Act.

7 Act of February 15, 1992 on Corporate Income Tax (Journal of Laws 2019, item 865), hereinafter: CIT Act.

8 For more on this subject, see: Chapter Three.

9 Act of November 20, 1998 on Flat-rate Income Tax on Selected Sources of Revenue of Natural Persons (Journal of Laws 2019, item 43 as amended), hereinafter: Flat-Rate Income Tax Act.

the indicated taxes comprehensively govern – we should point to the system of tax preferences related to agricultural activity or farmers in other taxes, which constitutes a departure from the standard taxation principles.

Separate taxation principles apply to farmers and agricultural activities as regards free forms of asset acquisition that are subject to **inheritance and donation tax.**[10] Notably, in addition to the standard instruments of this tax, which also affect farmers, the tax provides for tax preferences, which have a clear connection with the taxpayers' agricultural activity. They assume the form of tax exemptions for the acquisition of assets related to the creation or extension of an agricultural holding, rights of contribution to an agricultural production cooperative or group farming cooperative, and agricultural machinery and vehicles. These exemptions cover the critical legal and property elements related to the pursuit of agricultural activity and facilitate the free transfer of agricultural assets. Paid transfers of non-professional assets are subject to **tax on civil law transactions.**[11] Note that although the structure of this tax does not provide for separate taxation rules concerning agricultural activity, some elements of the tax structure indicate the possibility to take advantage of tax preferences. These preferences include tax exemptions (related, among other things, to agricultural insurance), or tax exemptions, mainly concerning the sale of land on an agricultural holding, provided that it meets the statutory conditions.

In Poland, assets related to agricultural activity and agricultural holdings may also be subject to **property tax.**[12] All real estate, except for agricultural land or forests, is subject to this tax unless it is occupied for business purposes. However, this exemption does not apply to buildings on land in perpetual usufruct, especially farm buildings located within an agricultural holding and used for economic activity or special agricultural production branches, buildings used by agricultural producer groups, other agricultural lands not located within an agricultural holding, uncultivated land, and land used for environmental purposes. For this agricultural real estate, there are statutory tax preferences in the form of exemptions. Moreover, commune councils may introduce other tax preferences in separate resolutions.[13]

10 Act of July 27, 1983 on Inheritance and Donation Tax (Journal of Laws 2019, item 1813 as amended), hereinafter: Inheritance and Donation Tax Act.

11 Act of September 9, 2000 on Civil Law Transactions Tax (Journal of Laws 2020, item 815 as amended), hereinafter: Civil Law Transactions Tax Act.

12 Art. 2–7 of the Act of January 12, 1991 on Taxes and Local Fees (Journal of Laws 2019, item 1170 as amended), hereinafter: Taxes and Local Fees Act.

13 For more on this subject, see: P. Pomorski, "Niektóre aspekty opodatkowania rolnictwa podatkiem od nieruchomości," in: *Opodatkowanie rolnictwa w Polsce. . .*, from p. 420.

Movable assets used for agricultural activity are means of transport, subject to a separate **tax on means of transport**.[14] Also in this tax, taxpayers who conduct agricultural activity benefit from tax exemptions for trailers and semi-trailers which, together with the motor vehicle, have a total permissible weight of more than 7 tons or more than 12 tons if they are exclusively connected with the agricultural activity of the agricultural tax payer.

Aside from direct revenue-income, income, and property taxes, including those connected with acquisition of property, we should refer separately to indirect taxes, such as value-added tax[15] and excise tax.[16]

The Polish **value-added tax**, subject to harmonization with EU law,[17] provides for a special procedure for flat-rate farmers.[18] The status of a flat-rate farmer depends both on one's supply of agricultural products from their own agricultural activity or the provision of agricultural services and on the exemption from value-added tax (which applies to farmers who are not active VAT payers). Moreover, it does not concern farmers who are obliged to keep accounts under other regulations. The specific legal and fiscal situation of flat-rate farmers results from their exclusion from many obligations incumbent on active VAT payers and the resulting additional obligations for those who purchase agricultural products from flat-rate farmers (obligation to issue VAT F-RF invoices). A flat-rate farmer who does not account for value-added tax is entitled to a flat-rate refund thereof. In Poland, the regulations in force, which take into consideration the specific nature of the flat-rate farmer's agricultural activity, give rise to many practical doubts, as seen both in the extensive case-law and the doctrine acquis.[19]

We should make a separate mention of **excise tax**, which, admittedly, does not have a special procedure or legal fiscal status for agricultural activity or farmers,

14 Art. 8–12b of the Taxes and Local Fees Act.

15 Act of March 11, 2004 on Value Added Tax (Journal of Laws 2020, item 106 as amended), hereinafter: VAT Act.

16 Act of December 6, 2008 on Excise Tax (Journal of Laws 2020, item 722 as amended), hereinafter: Excise Tax Act.

17 Council Directive 2006/112/EC of November 28, 2006 on the common system of value added tax (Official Journal of the European Union, L 347/1 as amended), hereinafter: Directive 2006/112/EC.

18 M. Duda-Hyz, "Szczególna procedura dla rolników ryczałtowych w podatku od towarów i usług," in: *Opodatkowanie rolnictwa w Polsce...*, from p. 257.

19 For more on this subject, see: M. Duda-Hyz, "Controversies over the status of flat-rate farmers in Polish Value Added Tax-selected issues," in: *Essential problems with taxation of agriculture*, eds. M. Burzec, P. Smoleń (Lublin, 2017), pp. 65–77.

but it includes tax exemptions whose analysis allows us to confirm the legislator's favorable approach to this activity. The tax preferences apply to farmers who sell dried tobacco and to taxable transactions involving coal and gas products intended for heating purposes within agricultural, horticultural, fish-farming, and forestry activities, and in households.[20] Note a separate tax preference, which consists in the reimbursement of excise duty included in the price of diesel used in agricultural production.[21] This mechanism is regulated in a separate law that implements EU regulations.[22]

II. The issue of tax subjectivity

In theory, the concept of tax subjectivity can have different definitions and forms. It usually employs personification or refers to specific legal entities (even subjective ones, such as inherited estate). In this context, we would find it difficult to create a universal theoretical model of taxable subjects. However, tax subjectivity always involves defining a particular set of rights and obligations specific to a given tax. The literature on the subject accurately highlights the fact that granting a particular person subjectivity in a given tax does not determine his or her subjectivity within the entire tax law.[23] Thus, within a specific tax, there may appear both typical subject categories also found in other taxes and original subject categories only characteristic of the given tax.

The abovementioned theoretical concepts find themselves intertwined in taxes on agricultural activity. Above all, the Polish tax law does not provide a universal definition of a taxpaying farmer. In principle, taxpayers who conduct agricultural activity represent all the forms of legal entities found in the law. These are

---

20 M. Münnich, "Podatek akcyzowy," in: *Opodatkowanie rolnictwa w Polsce...*, from p. 337.

21 For more on this subject, see: W. Miemiec, P. Pest, "The development of agricultural production and refund of excise tax," in: *Essential problems with taxation of agriculture...*, pp. 91–100; W. Miemiec, P. Pest, "Wykorzystywanie oleju napędowego do produkcji rolnej a zwrot podatku akcyzowego," *Kwartalnik Prawno-Finansowy*, No. 1 (2018), pp. 9–22.

22 Act of March 10, 2006 on the Reimbursement of Excise Tax Included in the Price of Diesel Used for Agricultural Production (Journal of Laws 2019, item 2188 as amended). Directive 2003/96/EC of October 27, 2003 restructuring the Community framework for the taxation of energy products and electricity (Official Journal of the European Union, L 283/51 as amended).

23 For more on this subject, see: M. Kalinowski, *Podmiotowość prawna podatnika* (Toruń, 1999).

natural persons, legal entities, and various organizational and legal units without legal personalities. In income taxes, the entity category determines whether the entity is subject to personal income tax or corporate income tax. A specific form of a tax entity appears in corporate income tax. It is a so-called **tax capital group**. This construction is exclusive to the tax in question; we can consider it as a certain tax preference. However, let us note that it does not only apply to those taxpayers who conduct agricultural activity. It applies to all subjects who cumulatively meet the statutory organizational and capital conditions, regardless of the economic activity that they conduct. This is also the case for another category of entities the tax provides for: the so-called **small taxpayers**. This status entails the privilege of lower taxation, which any entity subject to this tax can obtain.

Regardless of the above, however, the Polish tax law provides for **special regulations** concerning tax entities, addressed exclusively to the agricultural sector, specifically agricultural activity. In this context, we should mention a tax advantage related to excise tax. This solution, adopted in a separate Act,[24] consists in reimbursing farmers for the value of fuel excise tax. The Act implements the provisions of the EC Council Directive restructuring the Community framework for the taxation of energy products and electricity.[25] The main objective of the Act was to increase the competitiveness of Polish agricultural holdings on the European Union market and reduce the costs of agricultural production in Poland. The Act proposes a partial reimbursement of excise tax included in the price of diesel as a compensation for the economic burden of excise tax that farmers incur when they purchase diesel. To this end, it introduces a special entity – a so-called **agricultural producer**. An agricultural producer is a natural person, a legal person, or an organizational unit that owns an agricultural holding. Noteworthy, the Excise Tax Compensation Act does not include a separate definition of an agricultural holding and refers to the provisions of the Agricultural Tax Act in this respect.

Value-added tax provisions create a special form of taxable persons engaged in agricultural activity:[26] namely, a new category of **flat-rate farmers**. According

24 Act of March 10, 2006 on the Reimbursement of Excise Tax Included in the Price of Diesel Used for Agricultural Production (Journal of Laws 2015, item 1340).

25 See: Art. 6 of the Council Directive 2003/96/EC of October 27, 2003 restructuring the Community framework for the taxation of energy products and electricity (Official Journal of the European Union, L 283/51 as amended).

26 Act of March 11, 2004 on Value Added Tax (Journal of Laws 2020, item 106 as amended).

to the provisions of the VAT Act, flat-rate farmers are farmers who supply agricultural products from their agricultural activity or who provide agricultural service and benefit from the statutory exemption, except for farmers obliged to keep accounts. Within this category of taxpayers, the Act does not define the concept of a "farmer." Note that the value-added tax first appeared in the Polish tax law in 1993.[27] Due to concerns about rising food prices, the products of agriculture, horticulture, fishing, and forestry were exempted from the tax. For agriculture, the rate of 0 % was applied to the primary means of production. However, this legal situation was not favorable to farmers, who could not recover input tax included in the prices of goods and services that they purchased. Eventually, after several years, it was agreed that agricultural activity would, in principle, be subject to value-added tax, but would also have the possibility of a flat-rate system. When the new legislation came into force, all farmers acquired the flat-rate farmer status, except for those who were obliged to keep accounts. A particular procedure for flat-rate farmers appeared to compensate farmers for the tax burden included in the prices of certain goods and services that they acquired (these farmers benefitted from the exemption in relation to their supply of their agricultural products and services). Noteworthy, the above regulation is not exclusive to the Polish tax law: it naturally follows from EU regulations. Under the provisions of Directive 2006/112/EC on the common system of value-added tax, the status of a VAT taxable person depends on the person's exercise of economic activity: the concept of "economic activity" also covers agricultural activity.[28] Given the organizational problems that could arise as a result of imposing on farmers all the obligations to which VAT taxable persons are generally subject, Directive 2006/112/EC provides for the possibility to opt for a simplified taxation system, that is, the so-called flat-rate system of agricultural taxation. According to the preamble to Directive 2006/112/EC, Member States should remain free to apply a special procedure for farmers not covered by the general VAT scheme, which involves the application of flat-rate compensation for input VAT.[29]

The analysis of the regulations guiding taxation subjectivity within agricultural activity validates our theoretical assumptions mentioned in the introduction. In

27 Act of January 8, 1993 on Value Added Tax and Excise Tax (Journal of Laws 1993, No. 11, item 50 as amended).

28 Art. 9 of the Council Directive 2006/112/EC of November 28, 2006 on the common system of value added tax (Official Journal of the European Union, L 347/1 as amended), hereinafter: Directive 2006/112/EC.

29 Point 50 of the preamble to Directive 2006/112/EC.

essence, the Polish tax law does not provide a universal fiscal and legal definition of a farmer. The cited examples of specific solutions in this respect are exceptions to the general rule that establishes taxation uniformity of all tax entity categories. These exceptions are incidental, only specific to a given type of tax. All of them serve to introduce tax measures that constitute tax preferences for taxpayers who conduct agricultural activity. Therefore, rather than presenting a comprehensive, systemic approach to this issue, we should discuss solving specific issues within a single tax act, related to a given tax burden's legal nature. Although we do not question the need to maintain certain tax advantages for entities who conduct agricultural activity, we consider it justified to create a universal definition of an agricultural entrepreneur. We will attempt to formulate such a definition in the final part of this monograph.

III. The concept of agricultural activity

1. General remarks

An appropriate classification of given activities that a taxpayer performs results in certain consequences under tax law. Therefore, explaining the concept of agricultural activity proves crucial for further discussion: as a rule, income from agricultural activity is excluded from both personal income tax and corporate income tax. However, let us note that, under the Polish tax law, there are two very similar, yet slightly different, definitions of agricultural activity. The Polish legislator uses one definition of agricultural activity in personal income tax and corporate income tax and another, quite similar to the former, in the Agricultural Tax Act.

2. Definition of agricultural activity under the Personal Income Tax Act and Corporate Income Tax Act

The Personal Income Tax Act[30] and the Corporate Income Tax Act[31] define agricultural activity in the following way:

> activity that consists of producing unprocessed (natural) plant or animal products from own cultivation and animal breeding or raising activities, including breeding seed, nursery plants, breeding and reproductive material, ground, greenhouse, and foil vegetables, ornamental plants, mushrooms, and fruit; breeding and production of animal, bird, and commercial insect breeding stock of animals, factory-farming animal

30 Art. 2 section 2 of the PIT Act.

31 Art. 2 section 2 of the CIT Act.

production and fish breeding, and activities where the minimum retention periods for the animals and plants purchased, during which they are biologically active, are at least:

1. 1 month for plants;
2. 16 days for high-intensity specialized fattening of geese or ducks;
3. 6 weeks for other slaughter poultry;
4. 2 months for other animals, as of the date of purchase.

Given the above, agricultural activity consists of the following two independent activities: the production of unprocessed (natural) plant or animal products from own cultivation and animal breeding or raising activities, and the maintenance of purchased plants and animals for a certain biological growth period.

a) Production of animal or plant products

In order to understand what it means to produce unprocessed (natural) animal or plant products from own cultivation or breeding or raising animals, we must explain notions such as: crops, breeding, raising, animal or plant product, production, and unprocessed state, which the Polish legislator uses in the normative act.

Since there are no legal definitions for a vast majority of the abovementioned terms, under the Polish tax law and beyond, we find it necessary to make a linguistic interpretation. First, we should consider the term "cultivation." The dictionary of Polish contains three definitions, of which the most appropriate seems to be "a cycle of procedures from sowing or planting a plant until harvest."[32] Therefore, plant cultivation is a series of related activities undertaken by a specific entity, necessary for the existence and maintenance of the vegetation process. These activities end with the achievement of specific benefits. The term "breeding" is defined as the planned care for the growth and development of animals or plants, with particular attention to the specimens to be reproduced.[33] The term "raising" means "the rational maintenance and keeping of animals."[34] Therefore, let us note that the main difference between raising and

32 P. Skorupka, H. Anderska, Z. Łempicka (eds.), *Mały słownik języka polskiego* (Warsaw, 1968), p. 863.

33 P. Skorupka, H. Anderska, Z. Łempicka (eds.), *Mały słownik*. . ., p. 225. Moreover, let us note that the concept of breeding has a legal definition. According to Art. 2 point 4 of the Act of June 29, 2007 on the Organization of Breeding and Reproduction of Farm Animals (Journal of Laws 2017, item 2132), breeding is a set of measures aimed at improving the hereditary assumptions (genotype) of farm animals, which includes the assessment of the utility and breeding value of farm animals and selection of individuals for mating, conducted under proper raising conditions.

34 P. Skorupka, H. Anderska, Z. Łempicka (eds.), *Mały słownik*. . ., p. 78.

breeding is that raising consists in providing the animals with the right living and developmental conditions which often, but not always, allow them to grow biologically.[35] Thus, the process of raising comprises keeping the animal in appropriate conditions, feeding, and necessary care. However, it ends when the owner achieves the purpose for which he or she acquired and kept the animal (such as slaughter, natural death, or selling). Breeding is a broader term. Its scope encompasses not only rational maintenance and keeping of animals (i.e., raising), but also includes the appropriate selection of specimens to maintain and improve their commercial value, that is, their reproduction. Noteworthy, the Polish law considers the breeding or raising of any species as agricultural activity: even the breeding or raising of the most exotic animals, not commonly associated with agriculture. Examples include exotic birds (canaries, parrots), ornamental birds (peacocks, pheasants), amphibians (salamanders, newts), reptiles (geckos, turtles, chameleons, pythons), invertebrates (crayfish, aquarium shrimp, African snails, edible snails, scorpions, spiders, stick insects, house crickets, cockroaches and termites, locust), or small mammals (hamsters, guinea pigs, lesser jerboas). A similar remark also applies to the cultivation of plants (e.g. home-grown ornamental plants or aquarium plants). Moreover, it is important to note that breeding and raising animals or plant cultivation are considered as agricultural activities even if they occur outside of an agricultural holding[36] (e.g. in a flat or a house).

We should understand the term "production," which appears in the definition of agricultural activity, as taking specific measures to achieve the intended purpose: a plant or animal product. Note that production has close links with cultivation, breeding, and raising. It follows from these three activities. The plant or animal product itself may be unprocessed or have undergone preliminary or complete processing. Significantly, however, the legislator excluded the possibility of considering the manufacture of a processed animal or plant product as agricultural activity. Therefore, we should assume that an animal product is an unprocessed product obtained from animals that underwent a breeding or raising

35 This may happen if the farmer keeps juveniles for a longer time until they reach maturity. However, let us note that he or she may also purchase an adult animal, which will have specific functional characteristics (e.g. a purebred horse that participates in races). In this case, during the period of raising, it will not grow biologically.

36 The Polish tax law considers the following as an agricultural holding: an area of land classified in the land and building registry as agricultural land, with a total area exceeding 1 ha or 1 conversion ha. For more on the concept of agricultural holding under tax law, see: Chapter Four.

process. Such products may include, but are not limited to, milk, slaughter animals, eggs, feathers, hair, wax, honey, or wool. Also, animals intended for sale or further breeding or raising will be considered as animal products. In turn, a plant product is unprocessed plant material obtained from the cultivation process.

However, the legislator stipulated that the obtained plant or animal products must come from one's own cultivation, breeding, or raising activity. This condition means that the subjects should conduct the cultivation, breeding, or raising activity in question in their name and on their account.[37]

Many difficulties arise from the current definition of agricultural activity, according to which a manufactured plant or animal product obtained from cultivation, breeding, or raising must be unprocessed (natural). In this case, we should always consider whether obtaining a given product results from normal biological growth processes. In certain situations, this biological process is complete, but the agriculturist takes further steps to continue to produce plant or animal products. These situations include, among other things, drying plant products, freezing plant or animal products, grinding, or pre-treatment. According to the Polish dictionary, the word "processing" means "changing, transforming."[38] Processing gives a given product a different form and appearance. This definition means that a plant or animal product should be considered as produced in the course of agricultural activity provided it does not lose its initial state. Therefore, we should not regard waxing, stalk separating, and freezing fruit or milk as activities that fall outside the definition of economic activity since they are forms of storage of plant or animal products. Nor will this situation be affected by the necessity of using specialized mechanical equipment in freezing operations. Indeed, in these processes, agricultural products do not lose their original properties.[39] However, activities in which a plant or animal product loses its original form, such as slaughter combined with cutting,[40] grinding, slicing, cooking, stoning, pressing, or abrading plant seeds, do not fall within the definition of agricultural activity. In other words, when we note excessive human intervention

37 M. Burzec, "Pojęcie działalności rolniczej na gruncie ustawy o podatku dochodowym od osób fizycznych – wnioski de lege ferenda," *Przegląd Prawa Publicznego,* No. 10 (2017), from p. 55.

38 P. Skorupka, H. Anderska, Z. Łempicka (eds.), *Mały słownik*. . ., p. 660.

39 The same is true for direct sales of milk from specially designed machines, such as milk vending machines.

40 The judgment of the Supreme Administrative Court of May 20, 1998, ref. no. I SA/Gd 1422/96, CBOSA.

in the form of a plant or animal product, we should consider that it is no longer unprocessed (natural).

b) Keeping purchased animals or plants

The second part of the definition of agricultural activity comprises:

> activities where the minimum retention periods for the animals and plants purchased, during which they are biologically active, are at least:
>
> 1. 1 month for plants;
> 2. 16 days for high-intensity specialized fattening of geese or ducks;
> 3. 6 weeks for other slaughter poultry;
> 4. 2 months for other animals, as of the date of purchase.

To be considered as agricultural activity, the above operation must meet the following conditions. First of all, it must consist of keeping animals and plants purchased earlier. Second, biological growth should take place during the keeping of plants and animals. Third, the minimum retention period must be observed. Failure to meet the above conditions will result in the taxpayer's activity being classified as non-agricultural business activity.

The above regulations can raise numerous doubts. Note that the activity of keeping purchased animals during their biological growth period falls within the definition of raising. This inclusion results from the simple fact that the purchased animals are subjected to feeding processes, and their temporary owner keeps them in rooms intended for this purpose. Hence arises the fundamental question of whether we should distinguish the activity of keeping purchased animals during their biological growth period as a second component of the definition of agricultural activity. From a technical point of view, it seems sufficient to specify the minimum raising periods from the date of purchase. The legislator introduced the minimum retention periods for animals or plants in order to avoid situations where a given operator conducts short-term trade of purchased animals or plants (transactions) and refers to agricultural activity to gain preferential taxation, which we discuss in more detail in further chapters of this book. On the one hand, this provision is understandable. However, on the other hand, let us note that in the context of introducing innovative animal feeding solutions into agricultural production, the stipulated retention periods are too long in some instances. The best example is broiler poultry farming. According to the Polish law, the minimum retention period for slaughter poultry (including broilers) is six weeks. In contrast, in intensive raising, broilers are slaughtered as early as on the thirty-ninth day of their lives, often at the age of up to five weeks. Moreover, we should observe that the legislator counts the minimum period from the moment of acquisition. However, broilers experience the highest increase in muscle mass when they are about six weeks of age. Keeping these animals for extended periods generates higher costs and less income for the farmer.

The regulations related to the keeping of purchased plants also raise doubts. In this case, the purchase and subsequent keeping of plants, irrespective of the species concerned, for one month, during which they grow biologically, leads to such an activity being regarded as agricultural. Note that we can consider an earlier purchase of shrubs and ornamental trees and their subsequent resale after one month as agricultural activity. The same is true for ornamental plants used in fishkeeping.

3. Definition of agricultural activity under the Agricultural Tax Act

Within Polish tax law, we can also find a second definition of agricultural activity. It appears in the Agricultural Tax Law[41] and is used to impose an agricultural tax on land classified as agricultural land in the land and building registry.[42] The discussed Act considers agricultural activity as plant or animal production, including the production of breeding seed, nursery plants, breeding and reproductive material, ground, vegetables, ornamental plants, mushrooms, and fruit, breeding and production of animal, bird, and commercial insect breeding stock, factory-farming animal production and fish breeding.

Therefore, we should note that, first, the legislator uses the terms "plant production" and "animal production." In contrast, the definition contained in the Income Tax Acts employs the term "production of unprocessed (natural) plant or animal products from own cultivation or breeding or raising animals." Although these two terms are similar, they are not equivalent. This lack of clarity may lead to doubts as to whether an entity which conducts agricultural activity under personal income tax or corporate income tax also performs the same type of activity under the Agricultural Tax Act. In this context, we should clarify that the concept of agricultural activity contained in the Agricultural Tax Act is older, as the Act came into force on January 1, 1985. However, this conclusion does not change the fact that the Polish legislator should include a uniform definition of agricultural activity within a single branch of law: in this case, tax law. Thus, the terms "animal production" and "plant production" employed in the Agricultural Tax Law should be understood as the manufacture of plant and animal products

41 Art. 2 section 2 of the Agricultural Tax Act.

42 For more on this subject, see: Chapter Four.

through appropriate means of production to support biological growth processes.[43] Thus, we should understand the term "plant production" as plant cultivation, and "animal production" as breeding or raising animals. However, let us note that we did not explain the above terms based on the Act's literal wording. Namely, the legislator did not specify whether the production of plant or animal products within the legal framework of plant or animal production can occur only if its ultimate purpose is to generate an unprocessed product, or whether it can also consist in the partial processing of plant or animal products. Therefore, doubts arise as to whether a given activity that the taxpayer undertakes still falls within the definition of agricultural activity or whether it already is a form of economic activity.[44] A correct ruling in this respect has serious consequences under tax law. Specifically, land may be subject to agricultural tax if the taxpayer's actions fall within the definition of agricultural activity, or to property tax when it appears that the taxpayer's operations extend beyond this definition.

Second, in the Agricultural Tax Act, the legislator included the terms "fish breeding and raising." In contrast, the definition which appears in the Personal Income Tax and Corporate Income Tax Acts only mentions fish breeding. This inconsistency does not give rise to major legal consequences. As explained above, the term "breeding" has a broader scope, which should also cover animal raising activities.

Third, let us note that the purchase of animals and keeping them for the statutory biological growth period is considered to be agricultural activity. This action constitutes agricultural activity under income taxes. However, it does fall into the definition of agricultural activity included in the Agricultural Tax Act. Therefore, if the farmer conducts the abovementioned activity on land classified as agricultural land in the land building registry, then for some of his or her actions, doubts may arise as to whether such land should be subject to agricultural tax[45] or property tax, due to the recognition of this activity as economic activity (see Chapter Four for more information on the issue).

---

43 P. Meinberg, *Rachunkowość rolnicza* (Warsaw, 1971), p. 17.

44 For instance, in the judgment of Voivodeship Administrative Court in Szczecin of May 5, 2016, ref. no. I SA/Sz 222/16, CBOSA: the court ruled that gutting, beheading, refrigerating, and selling fish innards do not fall within the definition of agricultural activity. However, in the judgment of Voivodeship Administrative Court in Łódź of March 4, 2008, ref. no. I SA/Łd 1275/08, CBOSA, the court ruled that plant production is the activity of growing plants and possibly disposing of them. Plant production includes activities to prepare agricultural products for sale, but only those which do not involve product processing.

45 Art. 1 of the Agricultural Tax Act.

Given the above, we believe that the Polish tax system should include a single uniform definition of agricultural activity, which would play a vital role both under personal and corporate income taxes and the Agricultural Tax Act.

4. Activities that do not fall under the definition of agricultural activity under the Agricultural Tax Act, the Personal Income Tax Act, or the Corporate Income Tax Act

Noteworthy, taxpayers who engage in agricultural production tend to undertake activities similar to agricultural activity. In this case, doubts may arise as to whether their actions constitute agricultural activity. Note that due to the highly preferential principles of taxation of agricultural activity in Poland, from the taxpayer's point of view, it is highly desirable for a given activity to fall within the concept of agricultural activity, a matter which we will discuss in further chapters of the present book. This is particularly the case when taxpayers undertake additional activities that involve the use of fixed assets or livestock, closely related to agricultural activity.

First of all, we should note that income from the sale of fixed assets used in agricultural production does not constitute income from agricultural activity. This situation applies in particular to the sale of agricultural machinery (e.g. combine harvesters, agricultural tractors, trailers, seed drills, or plows). Indeed, the sale of these fixed assets, despite its clear association with the agricultural activity conducted, does not constitute income from agricultural activity, but only income related to that activity. The sale of agricultural land used for agricultural production is also not considered as agricultural activity. Notably, in the eyes of the law, the sale of land does not result from the sale of agricultural products. Therefore, under income taxes, the income thus obtained will be qualified as income from economic activity[46] under corporate income tax, or as income from the sale of real state or other property under personal income tax.[47]

46 The judgment of the Supreme Administrative Court of June 11, 2003, ref. no. I SA/Wr 3236/00, CBOSA.

47 Revenues from the sale of real estate or fixed assets will be included in this source of revenue if, from the moment of purchase of the property to its sale, the period of 5 years from the end of the calendar year of purchase does not expire. For other property, this period is 6 months from the day of purchase. The tax law provides for a tax exemption of revenue from the sale of agricultural land if it is part of an agricultural holding. Let us note, however, that if a taxpaying natural person runs specialized agricultural production, called special branches of agricultural production in Polish law, the sale of fixed assets will be subject to the same taxation principles as in the case of business activity (for more, see: Chapter Two).

The definition of agricultural activity is also not satisfied by farmers' services involving fixed assets (e.g. agricultural machinery, buildings) or animals. As a rule, the above activities fall within the concept of business activity.[48] Therefore, services aimed at intensifying or improving breeding and raising operations will not be classified as agricultural activities. In particular, these services include activities that are auxiliary to breeding and raising, which the livestock operators cannot perform directly due to their lack of knowledge, experience, or appropriate infrastructure. Such activities include, among other things: performing work to increase production efficiency, caring for core herds, introducing new feeding technologies, organizing groups of animals after the purchase of a herd, insemination, preparing animals for exhibitions and shows, hoof trimming, dehorning, dressing cattle, running an animal hotel or animal boarding services, or animal maintenance and care (e.g. preparing and administering feed, watering, grazing, ensuring the cleanliness of animals and their rooms, manual and mechanical milking, shearing dogs and sheep). Moreover, the definition of agricultural activity also excludes agricultural and horticultural machine work, which consists in performing agrotechnical treatments with the use of agricultural machinery, such as plowing, tilling, harrowing, rolling, spreading manure, distributing artificial fertilizers, sowing cereals and grass, planting crops, spraying plants with chemicals, mowing grass, harvesting cereals, digging up potatoes and beets, harvesting.

The rental of temporary accommodation in a residential building within an agricultural holding will also not fall into the definition of agricultural activity. However, let us note that, as an additional source of revenue, income from so-called rural tourism activity conducted by individual farmers is exempt from personal income tax.[49]

As explained above, the definition of agricultural activity includes activities which consist of producing unprocessed plant or animal products. Therefore,

---

48 When natural persons conduct such operations, they may be taxed either under a simplified method in the form of flat-rate tax on recorded revenue or under the general principles. For more on forms of income taxation of business activities conducted by natural persons, see: M. Burzec, P. Smoleń, *Introduction to Polish Tax Law* (Berlin-New York, 2018).

49 Art. 21 section 1 point 43 of the PIT Act. Nonetheless, to this end, certain conditions must be fulfilled. First of all, the rental can only take place in guest rooms located in residential buildings. Second, buildings with rooms for rental must be located in a rural area, on an agricultural holding. Third, the rooms can only be rented to people on holiday. Fourth, the number of rooms may not exceed five.

any activity of the taxpayer that involves changing the original purpose, characteristics, or consistency of the agricultural product should be considered as non-agricultural. Thus, any processing of plant or animal products from cultivation, breeding, or raising operations will result in classifying the revenue generated from these activities either as revenue from business activity or as revenue from other sources. The mode of production – traditional or industrial – is irrelevant in this case.[50] Thus, the definition excludes any activities consisting of, among other things, pickling plant products (e.g. producing haylage, cabbage, and pickled cucumbers), milk processing (production of rennin cheese, cottage cheese, yogurt), slaughtering and dressing animals for slaughter, including cutting, dividing, and classifying meat (pork, beef, lamb), producing wine (and perry or cider spirit) or traditional regional spirits from one's own vineyard or crops. We should note that this definition frequently impedes the development of agricultural activity. One example may be the situation of honey producers. The production of honey itself lies within the definition of agricultural activity, and thus the generated revenues will be taxed preferentially or not at all. However, if a given honey producer decides to add almonds, walnuts, or hazelnuts to his or her honey, this activity will no longer be considered agricultural under the Polish law.

IV. Final remarks

Our analysis leads to several key conclusions. First, the recapitulation of the principles of taxation of agricultural activity and farmers in Poland allows us to state that, in many aspects, the taxation system is preferential in this area. Nonetheless, there arise questions as to whether this system is built on modern foundations and taxation concepts or whether it is obsolete, whether it is appropriate and adequate for modern Polish agriculture, and whether it accounts for budgetary needs. In what follows, we will present detailed conclusions resulting from the analysis of Polish legal regulations in this area.

Second, a universal definition of agricultural entrepreneurs seems warranted, especially for the taxation of the income of entities who conduct agricultural activity. We will attempt to formulate such a definition in the final parts of this monograph.

50 Industrial processing will involve obtaining a given product through changing the original plant or animal product in such a way as to transform its form, character, or function. Moreover, let us note that such activity should be conducted on a mass scale with the use of mechanical devices.

Third, the Polish tax law should introduce a single definition of agricultural activity, applicable to the provisions of the Agricultural Tax Act, the Personal Income Tax Act, and the Corporate Income Tax Act. Moreover, the definition of agricultural activity should leave no doubts as to which real taxable transactions it covers. Noteworthy, in the future, if the legislator decides to tax revenue from agricultural activity with income tax, the definition should include the non-industrial processing of plant and animal products from one's own cultivation, breeding, and raising operations. At present, since agricultural activity is exempt from income tax, such an extension would lead to an even greater privilege of persons who exercise agricultural activity.

Chapter Two: Personal Income Tax

I. General remarks

In line with the Personal Income Tax Act, income from agricultural activity, except for special branches of agricultural production, is excluded from taxation. This exclusion means that, as a general rule, income from agricultural activity will not be subject to revenue tax. The only exception to the abovementioned principle is a situation where the taxpayer conducts specialized agricultural activity, called "special branches of agricultural production" in Poland. In this chapter, we discuss the principles of taxation of natural persons' income earned from specialized agricultural activity. In the Personal Income Tax Act, the legislator enumerated the types of cultivation, breeding, and raising activities that fall within the definition of special agricultural production branches. According to the Act, these are the following activities: cultivation in greenhouses and heated foil tunnels, cultivation of mushrooms and their mycelia, in vitro plant cultivation, breeding and raising of slaughter and laying poultry, poultry hatcheries, breeding and raising of fur and laboratory animals, breeding of earthworms, entomophages, and silkworms, apiary management, and breeding and raising of other animals outside of an agricultural holding.

II. The concept of special agricultural production - the grounds for a separate taxation system

The special branches of agricultural production appear in the personal income tax structure for two reasons. The first reason is the manner of land use. Let us note that, in traditional, non-specialized agricultural activities, agricultural land is treated as a means to produce goods such as plant or animal products. In this context, it is not only the quality and agricultural suitability that play a crucial role, but also the agricultural climate, water profiles, and topography. These conditions exert a significant influence on the achieved volume of agricultural production. However, the case is somewhat different for specialized agricultural production, where the land is not used as a means of production, but rather as a place of production. Within this type of agricultural production, factors such as soil quality, water profiles, and topography do not matter. The second reason for distinguishing between specialized and traditional agricultural production in taxation is the fact that theoretically, the former brings more income/revenue.

Still, it is important to emphasize that the profitability criterion should be no more than complementary. The profitability of specialized agriculture is a direct result of its independence from natural factors such as soil quality and climatic conditions, which eliminates the risk of losses incurred while conducting this type of activity. This risk-free profile results in a higher profitability of the agricultural holding which is the place of agricultural production.

Given the above, the question on the purpose of introducing separate taxation principles for specialized agricultural activity in the personal income tax structure remains. First of all, we must stress that the different treatment of specialized agricultural activities in taxation does not have a rational justification in those tax systems where income from agricultural activities is subject to income tax and the tax base is determined solely with the method of actual income determination through tax records (e.g. tax books). Moreover, the abovementioned distinction should also be absent from tax systems with simplified forms of determining the tax base for agricultural income, based on "internal" criteria, which account for the income earned or the income of a taxpayer who conducts agricultural activity. Such systems usually apply to situations where a taxpayer records his or her revenues, and the deductible costs are determined on a flat-rate basis (quotas, percentages, or coefficients). However, we should stress that the separation of specialized agricultural production from "traditional" agricultural activity will occur in those tax systems where the tax base is determined through external criteria, to maintain the correct principles of taxation of agricultural activity. This is the case in outdated tax structures, where revenue or income is determined based on a land's use-value (accounting for the land's soil quality value) or the cadastral value (a combination of the use-value with an average hypothetical income/revenue that a given land should theoretically generate). In the above constructions, the determination of profitability is only possible when the land is used as a means of production. Therefore, as we already indicated, such a criterion can only relate to traditional cultural activities. If the land serves as a place of production only, there is a need to determine the concept of specialized agricultural production and establish a different tax base. Otherwise, revenue/income from the above production will not be taxed or will only be taxed minimally.[1]

1 For more on this subject, see: M. Burzec, "Opodatkowanie dochodu osób fizycznych," in: *Opodatkowanie rolnictwa w Polsce…*, pp. 165–167; M. Burzec, "Taxation of specialist agricultural activity in Poland – an attempt to evaluate the existing solutions," in: *Essential problems with taxation of agriculture…*, pp. 52–54.

III. Scope of the special branches of agricultural production

The Polish law does not define special branches of agricultural production. The legislator only enumerates the types of cultivation, breeding, or raising operations that constitute this kind of production. We should bear in mind that only an activity that falls within the definition of agricultural activity can be considered a special agricultural production branch. The Personal Income Tax Act mentions the following specialized agricultural activities:[2] cultivation in greenhouses, regardless of whether they are heated, cultivation in foil tunnels, cultivation of mushrooms and their mycelia,[3] breeding of slaughter[4] and laying[5] poultry, poultry hatcheries (only chickens, geese, ducks, and turkeys), fur animals,[6] laboratory animals (only white mice and white rats), silkworms for cocoon production, bees (if the agriculturist has more than 80 colonies), in vitro plant cultivation, entomophagus and earthworm breeding, and the breeding and raising of other animals outside of an agricultural holding.[7] Classifying a given plant or animal production as a special agricultural branches occurs only when these cultivation, breeding, or raising activities are directly indicated as agricultural production branches,[8] and when their scope exceeds the statutory limits

2 Art. 2 section 3 of the PIT Act.

3 As long as the cultivation in tunnels and greenhouses and growing mushrooms and mycelia is conducted on an area of more than 25 m^2; otherwise, such production will be considered as traditional agricultural activity.

4 Only the raising of chickens, ducks, geese, and turkeys is considered to be agricultural production, provided that over 100 specimens are bred or raised.

5 If the breeding or raising operation involves over 80 specimens of laying hens in the reproductive stage, meat hens, geese, ducks, turkeys, and hens used for egg production.

6 Only the breeding and raising of foxes and raccoon dogs, minks, polecats, nutria, and rabbits (in this case, if the breeding and raising includes more than 50 female animals from the core herd).

7 The ordinance includes a closed list of animals whose breeding and raising outside of an agricultural holding constitutes specialized agricultural production. It enumerates the following animals: cows (over five specimens), calves (over ten specimens), slaughter cattle (over ten specimens), pigs for fattening (over 50 specimens), piglets and weaners (over 50 specimens), sheep for breeding or raising (over ten specimens), sheep for fattening (over fifteen specimens), slaughter horses, breeding horses, aquarium fish for breeding if the volume of the aquarium calculated based on the inner edge length exceeds 700 dm^3, and purebred dogs and cats.

8 This condition was stipulated in the yearly ordinance of the Minister of Finance, appended to the Personal Income Tax Act and the Corporate Income Tax Act. This means that only the cultivation, breeding, and raising of selected plant and animal

previsioned in the yearly ordinance of the Minister of Finances.[9] If these limits are not exceeded, a given breeding, raising, or cultivation activity will be considered as an agricultural activity and therefore, it will not be subject to income tax. The limits are the result of another criterion leading to the distinction between traditional and specialized agricultural activity. As we have already indicated, this limit is closely related to the criterion of higher profitability.

However, when we analyze the statutory cultivation, breeding, or raising volumes that qualify a given production as a special branch of agriculture, we can see that in many cases, there is no logical justification for the particular limit imposed. Moreover, the list of special agricultural branches itself is imprecise; as a result, a significant part of cultivation, breeding, and raising activities where land is only a place of production is completely exempt from taxation. This is the case in the breeding of exotic animals and the cultivation of exotic plants, also those used in fishkeeping. The same remark applies to special branches of agricultural activity (special branches of agricultural production) that consist of breeding and raising laboratory animals, where only the white rat and white mouse are seen as such in the eyes of the law. Such imprecision means that income from breeding other animals used for laboratory purposes (e.g. Japanese quails, rabbits, opossums, gerbils, guinea pigs) will be exempt from personal income tax. Similar doubts may arise when we consider the breeding of purebred dogs and cats, which is perceived as a special branch of agricultural activity only if is conducted outside of an agricultural holding. Note that in the breeding of the above animals, the land factor does not play a major role. Therefore, it appears that regardless of the location, the breeding of purebred dogs and cats should be considered as a special branch of agricultural production. The land factor also has no importance for the breeding and raising of one of the most common fish species in Poland, namely, the trout. Undoubtedly, livestock production that consists of trout breeding or raising should be classified under the special branches of agricultural production. This type of farming is usually run in small concrete tanks, and therefore, the land is only a place of production in this case. Similar problems arise in the area of aquaculture, an activity that is only beginning to develop in Poland. Due to the conditions in the Polish part of

species enumerated in the ordinance will be classified as specialized agricultural production and thus be subject to income tax.

9 If the normative limits are not exceeded, a given type of plant or animal production will continue to be treated as traditional agricultural activity and thus the generated income will not be subject to income tax. This is the case even if the land used for agricultural production is a place of production and not a means of production.

the seacoast, aquaculture uses artificial reservoirs located near the sea in order to ensure access to seawater.

The Personal Income Tax Act also creates other doubts, due to the legislator's imprecise definition of the types of breeding and raising activities considered as special agricultural production branches. One example is the breeding of entomophages, included in the list. As entomophages are a group of animals or plants that feed on adult insects or their larvae and pupae, several significant issues arise. In practice, entomophages are usually used in greenhouse cultivation: this group includes small insects or mites, such as phytoseiuli, midges, or Eurasian bugs *Orius*. However, in the current legal framework, since it does not specify which animals can be classified as entomophages, an issue may arise in the breeding of wild boards, woodpeckers, geckos, or tropical snakes that feed on insects. All the above animals are considered to be entomophages, but from a legal point of view, it is unclear whether they would be classified as such.

In this context, we should consider whether in general, animal breeding or raising, regardless of the location (within or outside of an agricultural holding), should simply be considered as a specialized agricultural activity. This suggestion seems justified since, in animal production, the land factor is much less significant than in plant production. We could argue that the connection between the land and the livestock is the fodder, which, depending on the type of breeding, is obtained from pastures, meadows, or crops (grain, fodder beet, maize). However, the land's use-value (soil quality value) has no direct influence on the animal production volume, increase in muscle mass, or potential income from breeding or raising. This is especially the case when a farmer possesses little agricultural land but conducts particularly intensive animal production. Thus, the land he or she owns cannot satisfy even a small part of the farmed or raised animals' nutritional needs.

IV. Determination of income from the special branches of agricultural production

1. The simplified income determination method

The taxpayer can determine their income from special branches of agricultural production with a simplified method: standard annual income estimates. Under the Personal Income Tax Act, taxpayers who intend to determine their income based on an annual income estimate should submit an appropriate declaration to the relevant tax office by January 20 of the tax year. The declaration should specify the types and volumes of intended agricultural production in the given tax year. Based on the declaration, the tax authority (head of the tax office) sets monthly advance PIT payments, with health insurance contributions deducted. However, if during the tax year, there are changes to the production, the taxpayer should notify the head of the relevant tax office within seven days. He or she is also required to do so if they cease or begin to operate facilities that enable a year-round production cycle or start operating special branches of agricultural production during the year.[10]

The taxable amount of the revenue of taxable persons who opt for the estimation method is established by multiplying the number of specimens,[11] area unit or volume unit,[12] by the relevant estimated median annual income[13] assigned to a specific cultivation, breeding, or raising activity. The Personal Income Tax Act presents the method of establishing cultivation areas or production units according to the type of cultivation, breeding, or raising activity. For greenhouse and foil tunnel cultivation, the median applies to every square meter of the total area, calculated from the internal wall length; for the cultivation of mushrooms and their mycelia, to every square meter of the area occupied by these crops. For aquarium fish breeding, it is 1 dm^3 of the aquarium volume, calculated from the internal edge length. For poultry hatcheries, it is one chick hatched. For laboratory animals, the unit is one specimen sold, based on contracts concluded for laboratory needs, research and scientific experiments, laboratory analyses and

10 Art. 43 section 1 of the PIT Act.

11 The number of specimens only applies to the following types of production: breeding and raising of slaughter poultry (over 100 specimens of chickens, geese, ducks, turkeys), laying poultry (over 80 specimens of geese, ducks, turkeys, laying and meat hens), poultry hatcheries (chickens, geese, ducks, turkeys), fur animals (over 50 specimens of foxes and raccoon dogs, minks, polecats, nutria, and rabbits), laboratory animals (white rats and white mice), breeding and raising of animals outside of an agricultural holding (over 5 specimens of cows, 10 specimens of calves, 10 specimens of slaughter cattle, 50 specimens of pigs for fattening, 50 specimens of piglets and weaners, 50 specimens of sheep for breeding or raising, 15 specimens of sheep for fattening, slaughter horses, breeding horses, breeding and raising of purebred dogs and cats).

12 The cultivation area unit for mushrooms and their mycelia, in vitro plants, greenhouse and foil tunnel cultivation is 1 m^2. This unit is also used for earthworm and entomophagus farming. An animal production unit is one specimen. One exception is aquarium fish breeding, where the production unit is 1 dm^3. The volume measure is also used to determine income from the production of silkworm cocoons.

13 Estimated median agricultural income that the Minister of Finance determines in the yearly ordinance, based on the price growth rate provided by the president of the Central Statistical Office.

tests, and control of technological processes. For the breeding and raising of animals outside of an agricultural holding, such as cows, calves, slaughter cattle, pigs for fattening, piglets and weaners, sheep, slaughter horses, the production unit is one animal sold. For the breeding or raising of other species, it is one core herd female for fur animals and one core herd specimen for breeding and raising of animals outside of an agricultural holding: one core herd specimen for purebred dogs, cats, and breeding horses, and one specimen for cows.

Two issues in the abovementioned regulations are worthy of note. First of all, it is important to note that a "core herd" is defined as the parent stock for breeding, used for several years. The core herd consists mainly of mothers but also adult males for reproduction. In this context, we should note that the legislator, when assigning an annual income estimate for the breeding and raising of fur animals, clarified that such an estimate is only established for females in the core herd. Thus, the estimated income is not established for males which may be part of the core herd and which are slaughtered after performing their reproductive function. Moreover, other females which are not intended for breeding will not be considered in the establishment of the estimated standard annual income. For the breeding and raising of purebred dogs and cats and breeding horses, the estimated standard annual income is calculated for each animal from the core herd. Therefore, both males and females will be included in the core herd. With these regulations in mind, we must draw attention to a certain inaccuracy in the existing legislation. This inaccuracy transpires when a taxable person raises a stallion outside of an agricultural holding. Such a situation raises a question about how to calculate an estimated standard annual income if this estimate is assigned to one specimen from the core herd. The problem is that a single animal cannot be considered a herd: according to the Polish dictionary, a herd is "a group of animals of a given species that live and are bred together."[14] Also rather imprecise and questionable are the provisions on the estimated standard annual income from poultry hatcheries. In this case, the estimate is calculated for one chick obtained from the hatchery. However, the Act does not indicate how to determine the annual income standard estimate when a chick hatches and dies after a few days.

The provisions of the Personal Income Tax Act indicate that if, during the annual production cycle, different crops, with different standards of income estimation, are grown on the same area, the income from each crop type is calculated based on the relevant standard. The standard is determined in proportion

---

14 S. Skorupka, H. Anderska, Z. Łempicka (eds.), *Mały słownik…*, p. 773.

to the number of months during which the crop was cultivated, including the preparation period. The above method of income calculation also applies in the event of commencement or cessation of conducting special agricultural production branches during the year. These solutions do not apply to cultivation in unheated greenhouses, where an annual standard applies regardless of the cultivation period and type.[15]

In most cases, income estimation through the abovementioned method is highly advantageous to taxpayers. Nevertheless, this method is not free of serious flaws, both for the taxpayers and the state's fiscal interests. From the perspective of the tax's fiscal function, introducing the principle of determining tax bases through annual standard income estimates is not beneficial as they are set at an extremely low level which does not reflect the actual income from a given plant or animal production. Moreover, let us note that annual standard income estimates may not be fair to the taxpayers either. This issue arises from the fact that the standards for estimating annual income vary too little depending on the production type and method. First of all, it is important to note the current rules guiding annual standard income estimates for greenhouse cultivation. Although the Polish legislator accounts for the differences in profitability among cultivation types, the division into ornamental plants and other crops is insufficient. Noteworthy, the concept of other crops includes too many arable crops to assign them all a single annual standard income estimate. In Poland, the structure of sheltered cultivation is dominated by three vegetable species (tomato, pepper, and cucumber), which account for 90 % of all areas under shelter. Profitability varies depending on the choice of crop species. Therefore, it seems appropriate to impose different standard estimates for species under sheltered cultivation and assign them individual annual income values. The case is similar for ornamental plants, where the income is different based on the cultivation type. Moreover, the way of conducting plant production also has a major impact on profitability. The Polish legislator made the profitability of crops dependent solely on whether they are grown in heated or unheated greenhouses. The annual standard income estimate for unheated and heated greenhouse production is PLN 2.60 and PLN 1.60 for 1 m^2 of crop area, respectively.[16] However, it went unnoticed that the profitability also depends on the type of soil: artificial or organic. The failure to account for the issues above leads to establishing the same annual

15 Art. 24 sections 4c, 4d, 4e of the PIT Act.

16 The annual standard income estimates for cultivation in heated tunnels is higher as production costs in such facilities are considerably lower.

standard income estimate for both modern and traditional greenhouse cultivation methods. These regulations appear unjustified. The legislator should introduce a distinction between crops grown on organic soil and those grown on artificial soil substrates. Each should be assigned a separate standard for estimating annual income.

2. The actual income determination method

A taxpayer who runs special branches of agricultural production may also establish his or her income based on the tax records kept, that is, the tax revenue and expense ledger and accounting books. In this case, income from special agricultural production branches is the difference between revenue from these branches and the tax deductible costs incurred, increased by the value of the growth in the herd of animals at the end of the tax year in comparison with the beginning of the year, decreased by the value of losses in the herd during the tax year. This regulation means that for income from special agricultural branches, the standard method of establishing revenue from the income source is excluded. Such solutions are to maintain the proportionality of revenues and incurred costs. They are to enable the cost of acquiring animals purchased in previous tax years to be taken into account for tax purposes, even if their sale took place during the year for which the income is determined.

The provisions of the Personal Income Tax Act oblige the taxpayer to notify the head of the relevant tax office about his or her intention to keep accounting books. The taxpayer should take such action before the beginning of the tax year, or before the commencement date if the operation of special agricultural production branches begins during the tax year.

To determine the income from an income source such as special agricultural production branches, there must be two essential elements, namely the income amount determination and the tax-deductible costs. The income amount can be determined based on tax records. Maintaining these records is tantamount to choosing the actual income establishment method. If a taxpayer decides to apply the above method, the amount of revenue from special agricultural production branches will be determined under the principles of determining revenue from business activity.[17] Thus, revenue from special agricultural production branches

17 See: Art. 15 of the PIT Act. According to Art. 5a point 6 of the PIT Act, a business activity is considered to be a gainful activity conducted in one's own name, regardless of its result, in an organized and continuous manner, from which revenues are not included in other revenue sources. Under the Personal Income Tax Act, gainful

will be the amount due, even if not actually received, excluding the value of returned goods and discounts. For taxpayers who sell goods and services subject to value added tax, revenue from sales is considered to be revenue reduced by this tax.[18] Additionally, the sum that the taxpayer obtained through paid disposal of fixed assets or intangible assets included in the register of fixed and intangible assets, used in special agricultural production branches, is also considered as revenue. This is also the case for assets on which taxpayers do not have to make depreciation and amortization write-offs and whose initial value is higher than PLN 1,500.00, and assets which, due to their expected period of use equal to or shorter than one year, are not classified as fixed or intangible assets.[19] The revenue can also be contractual penalties, write-downs, time-barred claims, and foreign exchange differences received by the entity who runs special branches of agricultural production.[20] Compensation obtained for damage to assets related to operating special agricultural production branches will also be subject to taxation.[21] The taxable revenue will also include the value of in-kind gratuitous allowances and other unpaid benefits. For entities who operate special agricultural production branches, this may be the case when the taxpayer uses agricultural machinery, storage buildings for machinery or agricultural products, or facilities associated with agricultural production, such as greenhouses, free of charge.[22] The revenue value is then determined based on market prices applied in the trade of goods or rights of the same type and category, taking into account, in particular, their condition and deterioration degree, and the time and place of their acquisition. However, let us note that in-kind gratuitous allowances and other unpaid benefits will not be considered as revenue if the taxpayers received them from their spouses, descendants, ascendants, stepsons, sons-in-law, daughters-in-law, siblings, stepfathers, stepmothers and fathers-in-law,

---

activities consist of manufacturing, construction, trade, services, exploration and extraction of minerals from deposits, and the use of goods and intangible assets.

18 Art. 14 section 1 of the PIT Act.

19 Art. 14 section 2, point 1 of the PIT Act. However, this revenue does not include revenue from paid disposal used for the needs of business activity and special agricultural production branches, right or share in the right to: a residential building, a residential unit which is a separate property, land, perpetual usufruct of land related to this building or unit, cooperative ownership right to a residential unit or a single-family house in a housing cooperative. See: Art. 14 section 2c of the PIT Act.

20 For more on this subject, see: Art. 14 section 2 of the PIT Act.

21 Art. 14 section 2, point 12 of the PIT Act.

22 Art. 14 section 2, point 8 of the PIT Act.

and also siblings' descendants, descendants of parents' siblings, stepchildren's descendants and spouses, siblings' spouses and the spouses' siblings, spouses of the spouses' siblings, and spouses of other descendants.[23]

In the determination of revenue from business activity or special agricultural production branches, the so-called "amount due" is crucial. The term refers to debt and payment, and describes nothing more than a kind of obligation to perform a payment. Therefore, we can say that an amount due is generated when the debtor's obligation to pay is due. We can only speak of revenue when the payment is due. At the same time, the moment of payment is not significant for the generation of revenue. The issue of the payment enforceability, i.e., the debt or, in other words, the revenue, is of major importance. In line with the Personal Income Tax Act, the date on which the revenue is generated is, as a rule, the date on which an item is issued, a property right is sold, a service is performed or partially performed, no later than the date on which the invoice is issued or the amounts due are settled.[24] For the generation of revenue from operating special agricultural production branches, the moment of payment has no importance. Given the above, we should ask whether, by way of exception, the revenue should be determined on the cash basis, instead of the accrual basis currently in force. The cash basis would protect entities who conduct agricultural activity (special agricultural production branches) from payment backlogs of agricultural product recipients. Noteworthy, the peculiar nature of agricultural production lies in its relatively long production cycles, which results in large time intervals between the investments and sales of agricultural products. Moreover, in the Polish conditions, agricultural production often requires pre-financing. Thus, in the event of possible taxation of income from agricultural activity, any delay in payment for agricultural products results in a deterioration of liquidity which makes tax payment impossible.

To benefit from the actual income establishment method, taxpayers who operate special agricultural production branches can choose one of two possibilities. According to the provisions of the Accounting Act, taxpayers may use the revenue and expense ledger or accounting books to determine their income.[25] Until December 31, 2015, taxpayers who did not submit their declaration of intent to keep accounting books could determine their income based on annual standard income estimates, regardless of the income amount generated. Such

23 Art. 21 section 1, point 125 of the PIT Act.
24 Art. 14 section 1c of the PIT Act.
25 Art. 15 section 1 of the PIT Act.

conditions were particularly beneficial for those taxpayers who operated large-scale special agricultural production branches. This beneficial character was due to the fact that their actual income was significantly higher than the estimated standard income, and, therefore, the tax burden on their special branches of agricultural production was low. According to new regulations, effective from January 21, 2016, if the obligation to keep accounting books results from the provisions of the Accounting Act, the income from special agricultural production branches is determined based on kept accounting books, under the principles related to income from non-agricultural business activity. In such a case, the taxpayers are not obliged to notify the head of the relevant tax office of their intent to keep accounting books.[26] The obligation to keep accounting books arises if net revenues from the sale of goods, products, and financial operations for the previous financial year amount to at least the Polish currency equivalent of EUR 2,000,000.00.[27] Note that if the taxpayer conducts economic activity in parallel to special agricultural production branches, only income obtained from special agricultural production branches will be taken into account for the above limit. The amount of income from non-agricultural business activity is irrelevant in this case.

Due to the low transparency of legal provisions, in this context, we consider as problematic a situation where the taxpayers simultaneously operate special agricultural production branches, in which revenues are subject to income tax, and traditional agricultural activities, in which revenues are exempt from income tax. The Personal Income Tax Act[28] stipulates that the obligation to keep accounting books applies to natural persons, civil law partnerships of natural persons, general partnerships of natural persons and partner companies, if their income for the previous year, under Article 14, which regulates the issue of income from business activity, was at least equivalent to the amount specified in the accounting regulations (EUR 2,000,000.00). Some fiscal institutions claim that in traditional agricultural activity and special agricultural production branches, when setting the limit indicated in the Accounting Act, the sum of obtained income should be taken into account.[29] However, such an interpretation appears to be erroneous. Given the fact that traditional agricultural activity is exempt from income tax,

26 Art. 15 section 2 of the PIT Act.

27 Art. 2 section 1, point 2 of the Act of September 29, 1994 on Accounting (Journal of Laws 2019, item 351 as amended), hereinafter: the Accounting Act.

28 Art. 24a section 4 of the PIT Act.

29 Individual tax ruling of October 28, 2016, ref. no. 1061-IPTPB1.4511.757.2016.1.DJD, www.sip.mf.gov.pl.

only income obtained from specialized agricultural activity should be considered to determine the limit indicated in the Accounting Act.

Note that the application of the abovementioned limit obliging the taxpayers to keep accounting books may be problematic when spouses who have joint marital property operate special agricultural production branches separately. For entities who have joint marital property, the general principle expressed in the Personal Income Tax Act applies, which states that spouses are subject to separate taxation on their income.[30] Thus, when setting the limit indicated in the Accounting Act, the income of spouses who operate special agricultural production branches separately should be determined based on the amounts they actually earn. However, in order to prevent the circumvention of tax law provisions, for entities who have joint marital property and operate special agricultural production branches, the limit indicated in the Accounting Act should consider the total income of both spouses. This is also the direction in which should go the possible changes in the Personal Income Tax Act.

3. Tax-deductible expenses

According to the PIT Act, a tax-deductible expense is defined as the cost incurred to earn revenue or to preserve or secure a source of revenue,[31] unless the legislator stipulates that certain expenses which the taxpayer incurs cannot be classified as tax-deductible costs.[32] For entities who operate special agricultural production branches, deductible costs are established on the same principles as for those entities who conduct non-agricultural business activity. However, if a taxpayer produces certain plant and animal products that are further used in agricultural production, the deductible cost amount should be determined based on the market prices applicable to the trade of goods or rights of the same kind and type. Moreover, it should account for the agricultural products' condition, deterioration level, and time and place of their acquisition.[33]

---

30 Art. 6 section 1 of the PIT Act.

31 Art. 22 section 1 of the PIT Act. See: P. Borszowski, M. Kowalska, "Podejmowanie działalności gospodarczej a definicja kosztów podatkowych", *Prawo i Podatki,* No. 2 (2009), pp. 7–10; A. Gomułowicz, *Prawna formuła kosztu podatkowego* (Warsaw, 2016); A. Gomułowicz, *Koszty uzyskania przychodów. Zasady ogólne* (Warsaw, 2005), from p. 13; A. Mariański, W. Nykiel, "Koszty w prawie bilansowym i podatkowym – pojęcie i zasady ich uznawania w zysku i dochodzie", *Kwartalnik Prawa Podatkowego,* No. 1 (2007), pp. 61–107.

32 See: Art. 23 of the PIT Act.

33 Compare Art. 22 section 6a of the PIT Act and Art. 11 of the PIT Act.

Taxpayers who operate special agricultural production branches depreciate fixed and intangible assets on the same principles as entities who conduct business activity. In line with the provisions of the Personal Income Tax Act, when taxpayers acquire fixed[34] or intangible assets[35] whose initial value exceeds PLN 10,000.00, they make a depreciation write-off. Noteworthy, in the eyes of the Polish law, assets which are not the taxpayers' property are also subject to depreciation, if they can use them to operate special agricultural production branches. They include, among other things, regardless of the expected utilization period: investments in third-party fixed assets accepted for use (renovation of farm buildings used to operate special agricultural production branches); buildings and constructions built on third-party land (e.g. poultry houses for breeding or raising poultry, greenhouses where ornamental plants or vegetables are grown), assets (fixed assets) that the taxpayer uses to operate special agricultural production branches, not classified as his property or co-property.

Under the Polish tax law, the following assets used to operate special agricultural production branches are not subject to depreciation: land and perpetual usufruct of land rights, residential buildings with cranes located on their premises, and residential units used for business activity or leased or rented based on a contract, if the taxpayer does not decide to depreciate them. Taxpayers may depreciate fixed or intangible assets with the following methods:

- **straight-line method**, which consists of making depreciation write-offs steadily during the period of depreciation. This is the basic depreciation method. Within this method, we can also distinguish the **accelerated straight-line method** for writing off fixed assets used in particular conditions (e.g. subjected to faster degradation, used in poor or unfavorable conditions). It consists of applying coefficients that increase the annual depreciation

---

34 Fixed assets include constructions, buildings, and units in separate ownership; machines, equipment, and means of transport, and other objects: owned or co-owned by the taxpayer; acquired or manufactured in-house; complete and fit for use on the date of acceptance for use; with an anticipated utilization period that exceeds one year; used by the taxpayers for business activity purposes or transferred to another entity for use based on a rental, tenancy, or lease contract.

35 Intangible assets include, among other things, cooperative ownership right to residential units, cooperative right to commercial units, copyrights or related property rights, licenses: acquired; suitable for commercial use on the date of acceptance for use; with an anticipated utilization period that exceeds one year; used by the taxpayer for business activity needs or transferred to another entity for use based on a license (sub-license), rental, tenancy, or lease contract.

rates. The taxpayer can also choose the **individual straight-line method** for fixed assets that were purchased as used or refurbished. In that case, the law stipulates minimum depreciation periods, the length of which depends on the fixed asset's value.

- **declining balance method**, which is applied to fixed assets that are special-purpose machinery and equipment, and all means of transport except passenger cars. It consists of increased depreciation write-offs in the initial years, as a result of an increase in depreciation rates, no more than twofold. When the value of the instalment to be written off becomes inferior to the instalment determined through the straight-line method, the taxpayer is obliged to make depreciation write-offs with the straight-line method.
- **one-off depreciation method**, which may be used by taxpayers who are in the initial stages of business operation or so-called small taxpayers.[36] One-off depreciation can only be made in the tax year when these assets were entered into the register; however, the total amount of depreciation write-offs calculated on a one-off basis may not exceed the PLN equivalent of EUR 50,000.00 in a single tax year.

Given the above, it is important to note that the Personal Income Tax Act does not provide any guidelines for the depreciation of the core herd used to operate special agricultural production branches. As already mentioned, the core herd is defined as adult specimens intended for breeding. The lack of guidelines results from the fact that the Polish tax law does not recognize livestock (animals) as fixed assets: only such a regulation would make depreciation necessary. We can consider this situation a kind of an unintended tax preference from the legislator's side. Note that while animals are not fixed assets under tax law, this issue is regulated differently under accounting law (balance sheet law). In line with the definition contained in the provisions of the Accounting Act, fixed assets are tangible fixed assets and their equivalents, with an expected economic utilization period of over one year, which are complete, fit for use, and intended for the entity's needs. These are particularly: real estate (including land, perpetual usufruct of land, constructions, and buildings, buildings under separate ownership, cooperative proprietary right to housing units and cooperative rights to business units); machinery, equipment, means of transport, and other goods; improvements in third-party fixed assets; livestock.[37] The very suggestion

36 Entities whose sales revenue (including the amount of VAT due) did not exceed the PLN equivalent of EUR 1,200,000.00 in the previous tax year.

37 Art. 3 section 1, point 15 of the Accounting Act.

to depreciate livestock under Polish tax law may come as a surprise to many experts in the field. This reaction is due to the fact that, as a rule, agricultural activity in Poland is exempt from income tax, except for special agricultural production branches. In European states where agricultural production is subject to income tax, livestock is treated equally to a fixed asset used in agricultural or economic activity. Therefore, it is completely natural to make depreciation write-offs for animals such as horses, cattle herds, or sheep. In Poland, special agricultural production branches, under tax law (if a given entity keeps tax books), are practically equated with non-agricultural business activity in the determination of revenues, tax-deductible costs, and the taxpayer's other formal obligations. Therefore, it appears that if animals are an ordinary means of production subject to deterioration in selected special agricultural production branches, they should be subject to depreciation if the core herd's value exceeds PLN 10.000.00. Of course, we assume that the legislator did not deliberately exclude livestock from fixed assets to favor those taxpayers who run specialized agricultural activity. The lack of legal solutions in this matter is rather due to the fact that the Polish tax law does not recognize the problem than to the desire to provide these taxpayers with preferential conditions.

An issue that may raise certain doubts is the depreciation method for a fixed asset used to operate special agricultural production branches, when income is estimated; if the income amount exceeds the limit specified in the Accounting Act, it is established based on accounting books. In such a case, it may be challenging to determine how to depreciate a fixed asset used for plant or animal production if it is not included in the fixed asset register. The law does not account for this possibility. The following aspects raise doubts in this respect. How should we determine the initial value of a fixed asset which was used for agricultural production during the period of special branch taxation through an annual estimate? By the same token, should the taxpayer take the fixed asset's initial value and then deduct the depreciation write-offs for the period of special branch taxation through an annual estimate? In the individual interpretations to date, tax authorities were favorable to the taxpayers.[38] According to these interpretations, the fixed assets' initial value should be determined based on the expenses which were actually incurred for their acquisition or production. Moreover, the taxpayers may include the assets' initial value in the fixed assets

38 Individual tax ruling of September 25, 2017, ref. no. 0112-KDIL3-3.4011.122.2017.1TW, www.sip.mf.gov.pl; individual tax ruling of September 25, 2017, ref. no. 0112-KDIL3-3.4011.118.2017.1.AK, www.sip.mf.gov.pl.

register, without deducting depreciation write-offs for the period of annual estimate special branch taxation. The above judgment results from the lack of appropriate provisions to regulate this matter. When the legislator obliged entities who operate special agricultural production branches to keep accounting books, he did not foresee the consequences for depreciation write-offs. Although, from the taxpayer's viewpoint, the above interpretations are favorable, it is important note that they may raise doubts in terms of the State's fiscal interests. Especially since an operator of special agricultural production branches who does not deduct depreciation write-offs made before introducing a fixed asset into the register obtains unjustified tax benefits. It appears that this issue would no longer exist if the taxpayer renounced the annual income estimate method for special branches of agricultural production. Therefore, the legislator should stipulate how to determine the value of a fixed asset, so as to leave as little room as possible for the tax authorities to make their own interpretations.

4. Determining the tax amount

As we indicated earlier, the revenue from special agricultural production branches can be determined in two ways: the simplified method (standard annual income estimate) or the actual income method (the taxpayer's tax documentation: revenue and expense ledger or accounting book). In income tax, the tax base is equivalent to income. However, the personal income tax provides for deductions from the tax base.

First of all, taxpayers can deduct **social security contributions** (e.g. for pensions). In Poland, they can pay such contributions to the Social Insurance Institution (ZUS) or the Agricultural Social Insurance Fund (KRUS) if the taxpayer is an agriculturist. Note that the sole fact of operating special agricultural production branches, that is, performing activities which fall within the concept of agricultural activity under tax law, does not necessarily mean that the taxpayer will pay pension contributions to the Agricultural Social Insurance Fund. Additionally, taxpayers are entitled to deduct payments into **an individual retirement security account** from their income. This tax preference applies if the taxpayer, of his or her own will, decides to save for his or her future pension outside of the compulsory public social security system. We should emphasize that operators of special agricultural production branches will be able to deduct from their income both the social security contributions paid and payments to an individual retirement security account, as long as they do not classify them as deductible costs beforehand.

Taxpayers who run special agricultural production branches are entitled to deduct their Internet use expenses, in the amount which does not exceed PLN 760 in a tax year. This deduction is only available to a taxpayer for two consecutive tax years, unless he or she benefited from this possibility in the period preceding those two years. The preference will not apply if the taxpayer classifies Internet expenses as deductible costs. In practice, taxpayers who conduct special agricultural production branches or business activity choose not to benefit from this deduction, as they find it more profitable to classify them as tax-deductible costs due to the lack of statutory expense limits.

Operators of special agricultural production branches are entitled to deduct **donations** from their income, which were made for the purposes of: religious worship; blood donation; public benefit organizations (e.g. foundations, associations); vocational training for public schools which provide such training under the Education Law. The deduction amount is limited: it may not exceed 6 % of the total income that the taxpayer acquired in a given tax year.

If the taxpayer is a person with disabilities or the financial supporter of a person with disabilities, he or she is entitled to deduct from his or her income the expenses incurred for **rehabilitation and facilitation of life activities** during the tax year. These expenses include, among other things: payment for a rehabilitation holiday; purchase of medicine; cost of a sign language interpreter; necessary transport for required therapeutic and rehabilitation procedures; maintenance of blind or visually impaired persons included in disability class II or I, and persons with reduced mobility included in disability class I, accompanied by an assistance dog. Most of the expenses above can be fully deducted. However, for some, the legislator provides for a limit, for instance, on the expenses incurred for the maintenance of an assistance dog (limit of PLN 2,280.00).

The income amount after the deduction of expenses is subject to the relevant tax rate, based on a progressive scale. In Poland, there are two tax rates under the progressive scale. Those taxpayers whose income does not exceed PLN 85,528.00 are subject to a 17 % tax rate. However, if their income exceeds the abovementioned amount, a rate of 32 % applies to the surplus.

Operators of special agricultural production branches who achieve high revenue in a tax year can benefit from the linear scale. In this case, the tax rate is 19 %. Let us note, however, that taxable persons who opt for the 19 % proportional scale will not be able to benefit from all the statutory deduction rights. They can only deduct social security contributions, payments to an individual retirement security account, and donations to vocational training for public schools which provide such training under the Education Law (no more than

6 % of their total income). The above deductions are available for taxpayers as long as they did not classify them as tax-deductible costs.[39]

Taxpayers who operate special agricultural production branches who calculated their income through the progressive tax scale or the linear scale (19 % tax rate) are entitled to reduce the tax amount by the amount of the **health insurance contribution** that they paid in a given tax year.[40] The health insurance contribution amount deducted from the tax cannot exceed 7.75 % of the basis for the determination of the contribution amount.

Those taxpayers who operate special branches of agricultural production and calculate their taxation based on a progressive tax scale, just as taxpayers who receive income from other sources, can reduce the tax amount by the so-called childcare relief. The above preference is granted for each minor in relation to whom the taxpayer exercised parental authority during the tax year or acted as the child's legal guardian if the child resided with him/her, or was the child's foster family. The deduction amount depends on the number of months when, during the tax year, the taxpayer exercised parental authority or the function of a legal guardian or carer and the number of children in question. For a single minor child, the deduction amount is PLN 92.67 per month, provided that the income of a married taxpayer and his or her spouse did not exceed PLN 112,000.00 in the tax year; if the taxpayer is unmarried, the limit amounts to PLN 56,000.00. If the above income limits are exceeded, there will be no childcare relief for a single child. In the case of two minors, the amount is PLN 92.67 per child; for three or more minors – PLN 92.67 for the first and second child, PLN 166.67 for the third child, and PLN 225.00 for the fourth and each subsequent child. Taxpayers who do not acquire sufficiently high income during the tax year, which makes it impossible for them to deduct the full amount of childcare relief, are entitled to a refund of the unused amount. However, the refund amount cannot be higher than the social security and health insurance contribution amounts that the taxpayer deducted in his or her annual tax return form.

Let us note that revenue from traditional agricultural activity is exempt from personal income tax. Thus, the preferences discussed above do not apply to persons who operate agricultural activity excluded from special agricultural production branches.

---

39 Art. 30c of the PIT Act.

40 P. Lenio, "Health Insurance Contributions of Farmers," in: *Essential Problems with Taxation of Agriculture…*, pp. 399–412.

V. Final remarks

The above discussion points to the necessity of indicating potential changes in the personal income tax structure. First, we consider it necessary to renounce standard annual income estimates. The consequence of abandoning this method will be the determination of income based on tax documentation, that is, the revenue and expense ledger or accounting book. Such a solution appears justified, as it will enable a greater taxation of breeding, raising, and cultivating those animal and plant species which, under the current regulations, are exempt both from agricultural and personal income tax (such as exotic animals). Removing standard annual income estimates means that the keeping and raising of animals and the cultivation of crops outside of an agricultural holding can be considered as special agricultural production branch. This will remove the necessity to name the animal species or crop types and assign them a particular standard annual income estimate. The income acquired from the special agricultural production branches will also reflect reality to a greater extent. The determination of the tax base through tax documentation will lead to greater differentiation in income from various types of cultivation and animal production. Under the current regulations, such level of differentiation is impossible to achieve. Second, we should raise the possibility of considering the breeding or raising of animals within the agricultural holding as a special branch of agricultural production. Thus, revenue from the breeding or raising of animals, regardless of whether these activities would take place within or outside of an agricultural holding, would be subject to income tax. As is well-known, animal production within an agricultural holding is subject to agricultural tax. However, we may observe a symbolic relationship between the taxpayers' land valuation classes and the income they obtain from the breeding or raising of animals. For this purpose, the legislator should organize the list of plant cultivation and animal breeding or raising activities which are classified as special agricultural production. A crucial criterion in this respect should be the manner of land use in agricultural production.

Chapter Three: Corporate Income Tax

I. General remarks

Current solutions on the taxation of the corporate income[1] from agricultural, i.e. traditional and specialist activity in Poland, are the result of the evolution of legal regulations and the changing economic situation of Polish agriculture. We can distinguish three successive stages of transformation: the interwar period, the Polish People's Republic period, and the pre-EU accession period, i.e. the transformation in the 1990s.[2] The factor that was undoubtedly significant for the current shape of corporate tax rules was the economic situation of Polish agriculture which, at the end of the twentieth century, went through intense structural shifts affecting, among other things, ownership rights. Initially, the transition from the centrally planned communist economy to the free market economy, together with the departure from state interventionism in agriculture, caused significant changes. First, a rapid collapse in agricultural production profitability. Second, the liquidation of the state-owned agricultural production sector and the privatization of its property. Third, the weakening of agricultural production cooperatives (APC).[3] As a result, individual farms used nearly 80 % of agricultural land, while the sector of corporate entities' holdings – mainly State Agricultural Farms (SAF) and agricultural cooperatives – was relatively insignificant.[4] To some extent, the process of SAFs' liquidation[5] enabled the development of the corporate entities' private holdings sector. Furthermore, corporate entities most often were organized into commercial partnerships with domestic, mixed,

---

1 CIT Act.

2 For more on this subject, see: B. Kucia-Guściora, "Opodatkowanie dochodu osób prawnych," in: *Opodatkowanie rolnictwa w Polsce…*, pp. 207–256.

3 W. Jóźwiak, W. Ziętara, *Zmiany zachodzące w gospodarstwach rolnych w latach 2002–2010* (Warsaw, 2013), p. 145.

4 W. Dzun, *Gospodarstwa rolne osób prawnych w procesie transformacji systemowej i integracji z UE* (Warsaw, 2015), p. 10; W. Guzewicz, A. Kagan, M. Zdzieborska, *Procesy dostosowawcze w rolniczych spółdzielniach produkcyjnych* (Warsaw, 2005), p. 39.

5 Act of October 19, 1991 on Agricultural Property of The Treasury Management (Journal of Laws 1991, No. 107, item 464, as amended).

and foreign capital.[6] At the same time, the property of SAFs was transferred to various legal entities, such as social and church organizations, associations, or foundations. Noteworthy, a large group of agricultural holdings functioning as a partnership with the State Treasury was formed from the earlier Agricultural Property Stock of the Treasury (APST). As a result, the sector of corporate entities' holdings became larger and diversified in terms of ownership form and area size. The years 1997–2003, i.e. the pre-accession period, were marked by an evident recession in legal entities' holdings, mainly due to a significant drop in the profitability of agricultural production, the problematic situation on the labor market, and the progressing privatization and decollectivization.

In the post-accession period, there was a significant revival in the development of legal entities' holdings. Certainly, the coverage of the sector by the Common Agricultural Policy (CAP) of the European Union caused the resurgence. Such circumstances influenced the quantity and area development of newly established legal entities' holdings, and the limited the decreasing number of existing state and cooperative farms.[7]

The tendency to improve agricultural productivity and farming efficiency significantly increased after Poland joined the European Union in 2004. Poles recognized covering Polish agriculture with the EU's CAP as an excellent opportunity for APCs. One of the most visible effects of European integration's impact on the APCs is the organization of these entities into the so-called cooperative groups of agricultural producers. The groups had access to the EU's aid for the development of agriculture, processing, and agricultural services.[8]

Surveys conducted by the Central Statistical Office of Poland after 2004 confirm that, in the structure of legal entities' holdings, large-area holdings dominate. After a significant recession in terms of quantity, accompanied by fundamental changes in the legal and organizational structure in the 1990s and the pre-accession period, the discussed sector grew economically with Poland's accession to the EU and the application of CAP to legal entities' holdings. The subject literature often goes as far as to emphasize that, as the farms of corporate entities progressively stabilize, their advantage in terms of productivity of land and labor, let alone efficiency of management, becomes increasingly clear.[9]

6 W. Dzun, *Państwowe gospodarstwa rolne w procesie przemian systemowych w Polsce* (Warsaw, 2005), pp. 300 ff.

7 W. Józwiak, W. Ziętara, *Zmiany zachodzące w gospodarstwach…*, p. 146.

8 M. Górka, M. Ruda, *Spółdzielcze formy gospodarowania…*, p. 237.

9 See: W. Dzun, *Gospodarstwa rolne…*, p. 238.

Given the above, we should contend that it was legal and economic aspects that justified tax preferences in the discussed historical period. However, it is doubtful whether the changes and strengthening of the economic and legal position considering legal entities occupied with an agricultural or mixed activity are justified at the moment and in the long term.

It seems that today's regulations do not correspond to the current diagnosis of corporate entities' economic position in the agricultural sector. We should consider the mentioned factors in the new model of agricultural taxation.

II. Taxpayers

The tax obligation in CIT concerns five categories of entities that generate gross or adjusted gross income covered by the tax in question. However, entities subject to CIT in the sector of agricultural-related activities pay the tax only for action in the field of agricultural production's special branches. In the current legal state, it is conditioned by tax exclusion of agricultural income.

Therefore, in terms of legal subjectivity, the first and the largest category of taxpayers are **corporate entities**, i.e. organizational units which obtain legal personality on the basis of legal provisions.[10] The way of gaining legal personality, the nature of business, its legal form or capital employed are not relevant to obtain the status of a CIT taxpayer. For instance, capital companies, stock corporations, limited liability companies, cooperatives, foundations, associations, or academic institutions can all be CIT taxpayers. The second category is **capital companies in the process of formation**, i.e. limited liability companies in the process of formation and joint-stock companies in the process of formation. Such corporations legally cease when the company enters the register of entrepreneurs in the National Court Register.[11] Until entering the register, corporations have the status of a corporate income taxpayer. Thanks to such a legal solution, both income and costs occurred in the period before the formal company establishment, i.e. before the acquisition of legal personality, are considered. The third category is **organizational units without legal personality**, except for companies without legal personality other than a limited joint-stock partnership. Since January 1, 2014, limited joint-stock partnerships

10 See: Art. 33 of Act of April 24, 1964 on Civil Code (Journal of Laws 2019, item 1145), hereinafter: Civil Code.

11 See: Art. 161 and 323 of Act of September 15, 2000 on Commercial Companies Code (Journal of Laws 2019, item 505).

with management or headquarters in the Republic of Poland are also CIT taxpayers.[12] The fourth category is **companies without legal personality that have the management or headquarters in another country** because, according to the tax law in their country, they are treated as legal persons subject to full tax liability.[13] The fifth category is the **tax capital group (TCG)**, which can become a separate taxpayer of CIT only having neither separate legal entity[14] nor the status of a taxpayer under other taxes.[15] TCG consists of at least two commercial companies that have legal personality and are in capital associations. The condition to obtain and maintain the status of CIT taxpayer by TCG is the cumulative fulfillment of organizational and capital requirements specified in the Act.[16]

If taxpayers – companies – meet statutory conditions and conduct an agricultural activity, TCG's formula does not exclude them from using tax privileges. The fact that the parent company and subsidiaries carry out agricultural activities excluded from CIT tax does not affect the possibility of establishing TCG. Similarly, the fact that the parent company and subsidiaries use remissions incidental to the CIT Act does not affect TCG's existence.[17] Since agricultural activity is not subject to the provisions of the CIT Act, conducting such an activity besides other activities does not exclude the TCG's provision's application. It is so because, in fact, we talk not about tax's remission but the lack of taxation. Therefore, companies forming TCG can be CIT taxpayers in connection with generating gross income also from non-agricultural activities. Consequently, if, after TCG's establishment, the parent company and subsidiaries continue to carry out agricultural activities, this should not affect TCG's functioning as long as it meets all other conditions.

Using TCG's structure is a very advantageous tax solution which may have the features of tax optimization in a situation when TCG includes companies

---

12 See: Art. 1 of Act of November 8, 2013 on Amending the Act on Corporate Income Tax, the Act on Personal Income Tax, and the Tonnage Tax Act (Journal of Laws 2013, item 1387).

13 E.g. French civil partnerships (*Société Civiles*) or general partnerships (*Société en Nom Collectif*).

14 See: A. Wrzesińska-Nowacka, "Podatkowa grupa kapitałowa w postępowaniu podatkowym," in: *Stanowienie i stosowanie prawa podatkowego. Procesowe prawo podatkowe*, eds. B. Kucia-Guściora, M. Munnich, A. Zdunek (Lublin, 2013), pp. 121 ff.

15 For more on this subject, see: J. Wierzejska, "Motywy tworzenia podatkowych grup kapitałowych," in: *Podatkowa grupa kapitałowa*, ed. A. Nowak (Warsaw, 2015), pp. 2–6.

16 Art. 1a of the CIT Act.

17 See: Individual tax ruling of June 2, 2017, ref. no. 0115-KDIT2-3.4010.43.2017.1.MJ, www.sip.mf.gov.pl.

generating both high income taxed with CIT, and companies generating high income non-taxed from the agricultural activity. For the income tax, the latter category of companies has no income. In TCGs, the tax determination based on the principle of cumulation consists in determining the income achieved in a tax year that is the surplus of all companies' incomes over losses. If the sum of losses exceeds the sum of companies' income for a tax year, the difference is the loss of TCG.[18] Therefore, the lack of taxable income – as it is from the agricultural activity – is a very favorable scenario for companies generating a taxable income. Thus, running tax-excluded agricultural activities can be the basis for optimizing taxation in terms of taxable income.

A CIT taxpayer can obtain the status of a **small taxpayer**, which entitles to use privileges in settling tax and a reduced 9 % tax rate.[19] A small taxpayer is a taxpayer whose value of sales revenue – together with the amount of VAT due – did not exceed the amount of €1,200,000.00 expressed in PLN in the previous tax year.[20]

The list of legal persons recognized as taxpayers is open, although it narrows when using the exemptions, including subjective exemptions regulated in Art. 6 of the CIT Act. However, none of the exclusions directly relates to entities conducting an agricultural activity or special branches of agricultural production.

III. Taxation rules for special branches of agricultural production

This study relies on a cumulative view of the subjective and objective scope of CIT presented below.

According to Art. 2 section 1, point 1 of the CIT Act, the provisions do not apply to the income from agricultural activities, except for the income from special branches. of the agricultural production. The CIT Act defines the concept of agricultural activity. Determining the scope of this concept is essential because the agricultural activity excludes from the discussed tax.[21]

The so-called special branches of agricultural production, which are subject to the principles of CIT, are in a different position. According to the CIT Act, special branches of the agricultural production are: greenhouse and heated

18 Art. 7a of the CIT Act.

19 A small taxpayer can use facilitating settlements not only for CIT (Art. 16k section 7; Art. 25 section 1b of CIT Act) and a 9 % tax rate in CIT (Art. 19 of the CIT Act).

20 See: Art. 4a point 10 of the CIT Act.

21 See: Chapter Four.

plastic tunnels crops, mushroom and mycelium crops, "in vitro" plants crops, farm breeding and raising of laying poultry and poultry for fattening, poultry brooders, breeding and raising laboratory and fur-bearing animals, earthworm breeding, entomophagous breeding, silkmoth breeding, hives keeping, and breeding and raising of other animals outside the farm. At the same time, breeding and raising of animals in sizes not exceeding those set out in Annex 2 do not constitute special branches of agricultural production. If the size of special branches of the agricultural production exceeds the values set in Annex 2, taxation concerns the income from the entire crops area or all production units in the tax year. Up to the sizes specified in the Annex, the Act treats special branches as agricultural production. However, if sizes exceed, all income is taxed immediately.

In the case of CIT, special branches of the agricultural production are taxed according to the rules applicable to other types of economic activity. According to the Accounting Act, legal entities conducting an economic activity must conduct accounting books. The CIT Act does not provide for taxation according to income estimation standards. Legal persons pay taxes according to actual revenues and costs. In the case of legal persons who must conduct a full accounting, it is possible to determine the real income and actual expenses of conducting business on the basis of accounting books.

The condition of the CIT taxation for special branches of the agricultural production is classifying the activity to one of the types provided by the Act, and exceeding the scope of activity indicated in Annex 2 to the CIT Act. At the same time, in the case of breeding and raising cattle, horses, pigs, aquarium fish, purebred dogs, and purebred cats, the Act requires meeting an additional condition apart from the size of the activity. Namely, conducting the activity outside the agricultural holding – in the understanding of the Agricultural Tax Act.

After fulfilling the conditions mentioned above, which allow classifying the given activity into special branches of agricultural production, income from the entire crop area or all production units in the tax year are subject to CIT.

Generally, the subject of CIT for special branches of agricultural production is described as **income**. The legislator does not provide for rules different from basic that determine the income. Particularly noteworthy, unlike individuals, CIT cannot determine the income using estimated profitability standards. Thus, as standard, income is the surplus of the revenues' sum over the costs of obtaining revenues achieved in the tax year, as in the case of other revenue sources. In a situation when costs of revenue exceed revenues' sum, the difference is called **loss**.

The CIT Act does not contain a definition of legal revenue. However, the Act indicates examples of revenue types, specifies the moment when revenue happens, as well as it specifies categories that cannot be the revenue.[22] In particular, revenues include: received money, monetary values, – including exchange rate differences – free or partially payable services, canceled or expired labilities, returned claims previously specified as uncollected or canceled and included in tax-deductible expenses, and so on. It is crucial to decide on the date of the revenue's reception to determine the revenue. The date associates with the moment when the tax obligation arises. Noteworthy, concerning business activities and special branches of the agricultural production, revenues are considered revenues due even if they were not received. In principle, the date when revenue happens is the date of item's delivery, disposal of the property right, performance of the service, or partial performance of the service, no later than the date of invoice or payment – the so-called accrual basis.[23] The Act allows the use of the so-called cash basis, which considers that the day of obtaining the revenue is the day of receiving the payment. The Act contains an enumerative list of cases when the acquisition of assets takes place, but it is not considered a tax revenue in the act's understanding.[24]

Tax-deductible expenses are a necessary category to determine the taxable income and, consequently, they affect the amount of tax. The CIT Act includes a general statutory definition, and fulfilling the criteria results in including expenses into tax costs.[25] On the other hand, the enumerative casuistic indication of what are the non-deductible tax expenses is a supplementation to the general rule. Consequently, we can state that the category of costs, as it is not in

22 In Art. 12 section 1, and section 4 of the CIT Act. Noteworthy, the CIT Act defines revenue much broader than the PIT Act.

23 As it results from the extensive jurisdiction of Polish administrative courts, there are quite a several problems related to the precise determination of the moment when revenue happens. See, among other things: the judgment of the Voivodeship Administrative Court in Warsaw of March 21, 2018, ref. no. III SA/Wa 1670/17, CBOSA; the judgment of the Supreme Administrative Court of November 10, 2016, ref. no. II FSK 1196/16, CBOSA; the judgment of the Voivodeship Administrative Court in Olsztyn of September 15, 2016, ref. no. I SA/Ol 393/16, CBOSA; the judgment of the Supreme Administrative Court of September 28, 2018, ref. no. II FSK 2655/16, CBOSA.

24 See: Art. 12 section 4 of the CIT Act.

25 See: Art. 15 of the CIT Act.

the closed catalog, includes any expenditure that meets the statutory conditions and is not in the negative catalog of non-deductible expenses. However, such an approach gives a wide field for interpretation. The general rule of classifying expenses as tax costs results from the normative definition. Expenses classify as tax-deductible if they:

a) incurred in order to generate revenues;
b) incurred to preserve or secure a source of income;
c) were not indicated in the closed catalog of non-tax-deductible expenses;[26]
d) were adequately documented.[27]

Polish legal literature and judicature emphasize the obligation to establish a causal relationship between cost and revenue.[28] However, the common practice of tax authorities consisting in concerning only the direct relationship between the cost and revenue raises justified doubts. It seems that it is also sufficient to reveal that the incurred expenditure could contribute to obtaining revenues.[29]

The issue of costs expresses the above-mentioned problem of the relationship between agricultural activity and special branches of agricultural production or non-agricultural activity. In such a situation, the CIT Act requires using proportion to demarcate costs of exempt, i.e. agricultural, activity, and costs of different provenience.[30] Therefore, agricultural activity should be separated in the accounting books in a manner ensuring to obtain the necessary data for the income tax. According to the tax authorities, the costs incurred by an enterprise that conducts agricultural and non-agricultural activities should be appropriately allocated to individual types of activity. Tax-deductible expenses from business should be included in the tax account. The costs associated with an agricultural activity should not be considered. Conducting both agricultural and economic activity by the taxpayer requires recognition in the accounting books in such a way as to separate revenues from the economic activity, revenues from the agricultural activity, and corresponding costs. Such a solution allows separating the

26 Art. 16 of the CIT Act.
27 Art. 16 of the CIT Act.
28 The judgment of the Voivodeship Administrative Court in Gliwice of October 5, 2017, ref. no. I SA/Gl 444/17, CBOSA.
29 The judgment of the Voivodeship Administrative Court in Olsztyn of December 20, 2017, ref. no. I SA/Ol 815/17, CBOSA.
30 Art. 15 section 2 and 2a of the CIT Act. The judgment of the Voivodeship Administrative Court in Warsaw of March 13, 2018, ref. no. III SA/Wa 303/18, CBOSA.

income from business activity – subject to the income tax – and the agricultural activity – free from the income tax.[31]

Tax-deductible expenses from the business activities should be included in the tax receipt. The opposite applies to costs incurred due to performing agricultural activities. In the case of direct costs, there is no problem with correct classification, as direct costs should be deduced in the tax year in which the corresponding revenue occurs.[32] However, doubts may arise in the case of costs other than those directly related to the revenue. If the taxpayer incurs tax-deductible costs from sources whose income is subject to the income tax and costs related to revenues from other sources, and it is not possible to determine the tax-deductible costs attributable to individual sources, such costs are determined in the proportion of revenue from those sources in the total amount of revenue.[33] This rule also applies if the taxpayer incurs tax-deductible costs from sources from which part of the income is not subject to the income tax or is exempt from such tax.[34]

There are specific rules for determining the value of raw materials and resources that come from own crop and animal production, and own forestry, used in agricultural and food processing, or in special branches of agricultural production.[35] In such a situation, the value of obtained goods or rights, including those received free of charge, should be determined on the basis of the market prices applicable to trade in goods or rights of the same type. Moreover, goods and rights should be considered in terms of condition, degree of usage, and the time and place of acquisition.[36]

One of the conditions to classify expenses as tax-deductible is not to put them in the negative catalog of non-deductible expenses.[37] The standard rules of these exclusions apply to the special branches of agricultural production, and, therefore, we will omit them. However, it is worth noting the new regulation introduced since 2017 that relates to the rules of classifying expenses as tax-deductible. According to the rule, taxpayers cannot recognize an expense

---

31 Art. 9 of the CIT Act.
32 Art. 15 section 4 of the CIT Act.
33 Art. 15 section 2 and 2a of the CIT Act.
34 Individual tax ruling of January 25, 2011, ref. no. IPPB5/423-730/10-6/DG, www.sip.mf.gov.pl.
35 Art. 15 section 3 of the CIT Act.
36 Art. 12 section 5 of the CIT Act.
37 Art. 16 of the CIT Act.

deductible if the payment concerning the performed business activity was made without the intermediation of a payment account.

If tax-deductible expenses exceed the sum of revenues, the difference is a **loss**. The amount of the loss incurred in a tax year may be reduced with the amount of income in the following five consecutive tax years. The amount of reduction in any year may not exceed 50 % of the loss. Such rules also apply as a standard to taxpayers running special branches of agricultural production. We can assess the rules as a type of tax preference for this group of taxpayers.

Due to the actual open state of CIT, the income or loss from special branches of agricultural production is determined for the settlement period, i.e. the **tax year**. The rule is that the tax year is a calendar year. However, a taxpayer may decide of different 12 consecutive months to be the tax year. Accepting a separate designation of the tax year requires appropriate regulations in the statute, partnership agreement, or other document regulating the taxpayer's systematic rules. However, a necessary condition for accepting a different period of the tax year is to notify the head of the tax office within a statutory deadline. In the case of changing the tax year or starting an activity during the year, the Act regulates special transitional rules that extend or shorten the tax year.[38]

The correct determination of the income or loss from special branches of agricultural activity as well as the tax base and, consequently, the amount of tax, requires taxpayers to keep accounting records under the principles set in the Accounting Act.[39] Moreover, taxpayers running special branches of agricultural production are obliged to keep records of fixed and intangible assets. Noteworthy, the regulations on accounting specify only the manner of maintaining accounting records. However, the rules cannot be the basis to adopt tax rules different from those set in the CIT Act.[40] If it is not possible to determine the income or loss[41] based on accounting books, they ought to be determined by estimation. The CIT Act requires to apply an income indicator in relation to the revenue of, in this case, 20 % only if learning the income from special branches of agricultural production refers to non-residents. The 20 % indicator comes from the fact that special branches of agricultural production are not explicitly listed with any of the statutory indicators; thus, they should be treated as other activities.[42]

38 See: Art. 8 section 2 and 2a of the CIT Act.

39 See: Art. 2 of the Accounting Act.

40 See: The judgment of the Voivodeship Administrative Court in Warsaw of March 26, 2007, ref. no. III SA/Wa 2431/06, CBOSA.

41 See: Art. 24 of the Accounting Act.

42 Art. 9 section 2a of the CIT Act.

Regarding special branches of agricultural production, the tax base is the income which may be reduced by tax exemptions at the stage of determining the annual tax. There are not many CIT exemptions, and none of them is a preference dedicated exclusively to special branches of agricultural production.[43]

General rules for setting tax rates apply to the special branches of agricultural production. The **19 % rate**, which refers to the tax base, i.e. the **income**, is essential. A new 15 % stake of the tax base rate was introduced on January 1, 2017, and then it was reduced to a 9 % rate, beginning with 2019. However, the lower rate is not generally applicable. It was designed only for selected groups of taxpayers: small taxpayers, and taxpayers who start their activity. Moreover, TCG cannot benefit from the 9 % rate.

As a rule, the settlement period in the CIT is a tax year. Therefore, the final settlement of the tax regarding taxpayers obtaining income from special branches of agricultural production takes place after tax year's end. However, taxpayers are obliged to pay advances to the account of the competent tax authority during the year. As a rule, **advances** are made for monthly periods by the twentieth day of each month for the previous month. In some situations, it is possible to make advance payments for **quarter periods** by the twentieth day of the month following the quarter. Such a rule applies to small taxpayers and taxpayers commencing their activity in the first tax year. Taxpayers may also choose a simplified form of advance payment in the **amount of 1/12** of the due tax indicated in the tax return for the previous tax year. Taxpayers obtaining income from special branches of agricultural production are not exempt from paying CIT advances.

As a rule, taxpayers must settle the annual tax in their **tax return**. Taxpayers submit tax returns **by the end of the third month** of the following tax year. Within this deadline, taxpayers must pay the tax resulting from the tax return after comparing the amount of tax due and the sum of advance payments made during the year. Besides the obligation to submit an annual tax return, taxpayers must prepare a financial statement and submit it to the tax authority together with the opinion and report of the entity authorized to audit financial statements within ten days from the annual report's approval. Additionally, partnerships attach a copy of the partners' or shareholders' meeting resolution approving the yearly financial report.

43 It seems that both exemptions for donations for public benefit or religious cult purposes – according to Art. 18 of the CIT Act – as well as for the so-called eligible costs, i.e., expenses incurred by the taxpayer because of research and development activities – according to Art. 18d of the CIT Act – are tax-deductible.

A legal person withdrawing the dividend from the agricultural activity income does not collect the tax on the withdrawn dividend. However, a legal person running a special branches of agricultural production or a non-agricultural activity besides an agricultural activity must collect a tax of 19 % of the revenue obtained.[44] Noteworthy, under statutory conditions, in such a case, it is possible to take advantage of the exemption from taxation of dividends paid to both residents and non-residents with a legal address in EU, EEA, or the Swiss Confederation, which is compatible with European Union law.[45]

To sum up, we can say that the structure of CIT in terms of taxation of special branches of agricultural activity's income does not deviate from the standard rule of taxation for other taxpayers.

Such an approach supports the concept of treating this category of taxpayers with a principle of universal subjectivity. Also, the approach confirms that a legal person or an organizational unit without a legal personality running special branches of agricultural production is subject to general rules of taxation. However, general rules should also be extended to taxpayers running an agricultural activity with a simultaneous resignation from the agricultural tax for the benefit of property tax on owned land, on which the activity is run.

IV. Tax preferences

1. The general characteristic of preferences

Polish CIT provides several tax exemptions, which are tax preferences. Preferences' number and frequent changes result in constant modifications in the catalog. Below we present only selected CIT exemptions with a clear agricultural context, or those which apply to entities running an agricultural activity or an activity related to it despite the lack of a clearly agricultural background. The specificity of all discussed tax preferences is that their legal and financial effects concern entities whose agricultural activity is subject to a tax exemption – which, in the Polish tax system, may be considered a super-preference. However, the legislator promotes tax entities showing certain links with agriculture by dedicating special exemptions for income coming from other sources, yet related subjectively or objectively to agricultural activity.

44 Art. 22 of the CIT Act.

45 Council Directive 2011/96/UE of November 30, 2011 on the common system of taxation applicable in the case of parent companies and subsidiaries in different member states (Official Journal of the European Union, L 345/8 as amended).

2. Exemption of the income from selling of real estate which belongs to an agricultural holding

The income from selling of real estate, in whole or part, is tax free as long as the real estate in question belongs to an agricultural holding. However, the exemption does not apply to the income from the sale if it takes place within five years, counting from the end of the calendar year in which the real estate, in whole or part, was acquired.[46]

Applying the exemption requires that the sale takes place five years after the end of the real estate's acquisition year. Moreover, viewing the Agricultural Tax Act's provisions, the sale may not concern land seized for business activities other than the agricultural one. Applying the definition of the agricultural holding in the Agricultural Tax Act's understanding is crucial to recognize the real estate as a part of the holding.[47] Therefore, it is vital whether the land constitutes an agricultural area, is wooded and bushed land in the agricultural area, or whether it is a built-up agricultural area. The primary condition for recognizing area as a holding is its size, defined as a territorial norm. If the total size of land exceeds one hectare of an agricultural area, wooded and bushed area, or one conversion hectare of the agricultural area, the land is an agricultural holding in the understanding of the Agricultural Tax Act's Art. 2. If the land does not meet the territorial norm, it cannot be recognized as an agricultural holding because the only component of an agricultural holding in the understanding of the Agricultural Tax Act is area of total size exceeding one ha or one conversion ha. At the same time, not all types of land which meet the up-mentioned standards are part of an agricultural holding in the understanding of the Agricultural Tax Act. The area of an agricultural holding does not include land occupied for business activity other than an agricultural one, or a forest area.[48]

The CIT Act does not make the right to take advantage of the questioned exemption dependent on whether the entity selling the agricultural holding conducts an agricultural activity in person. Such an interpretation is essential for taxpayers who lease their agricultural holding. Owners do not run an agricultural activity; thus, under a lease agreement, they have the right to transfer the use and collection of benefits from the questioned real estate in return for the rent settled in the agreement to the lessee. The lessee runs an agricultural

---

46 Art. 17 section 1, point 1 of the CIT Act.

47 Art. 2 section 4 of the CIT Act in relation to Art. 1 and 2 of the Agricultural Tax Act.

48 Individual tax ruling of October 28, 2019, ref. no. 0111-KDIB1-1.4010.338.2019.2.BSA, www.sip.mf.gov.pl.

activity on the property. It is sufficient when the given area is recognized as an agricultural holding to benefit from the mentioned exemption. Also, the interested entity must own agricultural areas that are independent or dependent possessions, and it is not necessary to obtain income from them. Therefore, cessation of activity or reduction of agricultural production in a given area does not automatically result in losing the status of an agricultural holding.[49] The other conditions entitling to the exemption require referring to the civil law understanding of the sales contract.[50]

Polish courts concentrate on the fact that in a situation where the agricultural area is the element of an enterprise or its organized part, at the same time, it can be a real estate constituting an agricultural holding in the understanding of Art. 2 section 4 of the CIT Act. Therefore, the examination of such properties' features and clarification, whether they were a part of an agricultural holding in the CIT Act's understanding, is a crucial element to the mentioned provisions' interpretation.[51]

3. Tax preferences for an agricultural producers' group

The exemption of income for agricultural producers' group in the register is a significant preference in CIT.[52] The income must come from the sale of products, or groups of products, for which the group exists. Products must be produced in the group's member's holdings – in part spent on behalf of the group's members in the tax year or the following year.[53]

Since 2000, the Polish legislation provides for the possibility of organizing agricultural producers in the so-called Agricultural Producer Groups (APG).[54]

---

49 The judgment of the Voivodeship Administrative Court in Wrocław of March 6, 2008, ref. no. I SA/Wr 202/08, CBOSA. Individual tax ruling of June 27, 2019, ref. no. 0111-KDIB1-1.4010.178.2019.2.MF, www.sip.mf.gov.pl.

50 Art. 46–48 and 535 of the Civil Code.

51 Individual tax ruling of July 30, 2019, ref. no. 0111-KDIB2-1.4010.230.2019.2.AP, https://sip.mf.gov.pl; the judgment of the Supreme Administrative Court of April 28, 2016, ref. no. II FSK 671/14, CBOSA; the judgment of the Voivodeship Administrative Court in Opole of November 20, 2013, ref. no. I SA/Op 482/13, CBOSA.

52 More in: B. Kucia-Guściora, "Węzłowe problemy preferencji podatkowych dla grup producentów rolnych," *Wieś i Rolnictwo*, 2019, No. 1, pp. 25–44.

53 Art. 17 section 1, point 49 of the CIT Act.

54 Act of September 15, 2000 on Agricultural Producer Groups, Their Connections and About Other Acts' Change (Journal of Laws 2018, item 1028), hereinafter: the APG Act.

Natural persons, organizational units without legal personality, as well as legal persons who run an agricultural holding in the understanding of the Agricultural Tax Act[55] or a special branch of agricultural production, can constitute APGs.[56] Noteworthy, the understanding of the agricultural activity concept provided by the APG Act was adopted under EU's rules and means production, breeding or cultivation of agricultural products including harvesting, milking, breeding and keeping animals for farming purposes.[57]

Essential conditions for creating APG and its functioning include legal stipulations concerning the group's entity structure. The group may be created by producers of one agricultural product or a group of products, provided that the main objective of creating the group is realized.[58] Moreover, the subjective structure of the group assumes exclusivity, i.e. each member belongs just to one group regarding a given product or group of products. Entity conditions also connect with the shareholding structure in the group of agricultural producers.[59]

APG's functioning also depends on economic considerations. Besides, the group has to set rules for members concerning the quality and quantity of products or groups of products, and methods of preparing products for sale. The Act requires that annual revenues from the sale of products or groups of products produced in agricultural holdings or special branches of the agricultural production of group's members constitute more than half of the group's revenues from the sale of products or groups of products due to which the group established. Moreover, participating in the group of agricultural producers connects with each member's obligation to annually sell at least 80 % of products – due to which the group exists – to the group. However, the latter condition does not hold when the lack of production is due to force majeure or exceptional circumstances.[60]

---

55 Art. 2 of the Agricultural Tax Act.

56 Art. 2 of the CIT Act.

57 Art. 4 section 1, letter c, point I of the European Parliament's and EU Council's resolution No. 1307/2013 of December 17, 2013 on establishing rules for direct payments to farmers under support systems within the common agricultural policy, and repealing EC Council's resolution No. 73/2009 (Official Journal of the European Union L 347/608 as amended).

58 The judgment of the Voivodeship Administrative Court in Warsaw of April 11, 2011, ref. no. V SA/Wa 2298/10, CBOSA.

59 More in: B. Kucia-Guściora, "Agricultural producer groups in Polish Corporate Income Tax," in: *Essential problems with taxation of agriculture…*, pp. 23–36.

60 See: Art. 2 section 2 of the European Parliament's and EU Council's resolution No. 1306/2013 of December 17, 2013 on financing, management, and monitoring of

APG, due to its legal status, i.e. an entrepreneur with a legal personality, is subject to CIT.[61] The specificity of agricultural producers' group's taxation relates to the fact that members run agricultural activity – the revenue then is not subject to CIT – or the so-called special branches of agricultural production, which are subject to CIT. The main objective of APG is running neither agricultural activity nor special branches of agricultural production. We can state that agricultural producers organize themselves in groups that have a separate legal personality due to the group's auxiliary activity character toward its members. Therefore, the group, remaining in close connection with the farmer's activity, allows him to participate in further stages of agricultural product trade, thus improving farmer's profitability.

General principles of APG's CIT taxation are not different from the adopted taxation standard. However, the tax legislation provides for significant exceptions to the up-mentioned standard resulting from the list of exemptions in question.

The exemption meant explicitly for APGs is of particular importance. Exemption's legal structure significantly modifies the indicated taxation standard. The questioned exemption is subjective and conditional in nature. The regulations mentioned above establish three material and legal premises for including the income of a CIT payer in the exemption.

The first premise refers to the status of the taxpayer. Obtaining the status of an APG by the taxpayer is a necessary condition of a subjective character. From the formal-legal point of view, a group of agricultural producers acts on the basis of a founding act, which may have the form of a statute or agreement. The content of the founding act should comply with statutory requirements. The procedure of recognition or refusal of recognition of an APG is of administrative and legal nature. As in the case of approving the business plan,[62] it is the director of the Agency for Restructuring and Modernization of Agriculture (ARMA) relevant to the group's seat who recognizes the group.[63] Recognized agricultural producer groups are subject to registration. The director of the local ARMA branch relevant to the group's seat runs the register of groups.

---

the common agricultural policy, and repealing EEC Council's resolution No. 352/78, (EC) No. 165/94, (EC) No. 2799/98, (EC) No. 814/2000, (EC) No. 1290/2005, and (EC) No. 485/2008 (Official Journal of the European Union L 347/549).

61 See: Art. 1 of the CIT Act.

62 Regulation of the Minister of Agriculture and Rural Development of February 18, 2016 on the requirements to be met by the business plan of an agricultural producers' group (Journal of Laws 2016, item 237).

63 Art. 7 of the APG Act.

The second premise is of an objective nature as it relates to the source of income obtained by the group. The exemption was limited to income received from a specific type of activity, i.e. the sale of products or groups of products due to which APG established. Moreover, the products or groups of products must be produced in members' agricultural holdings, which is very important from the objective point of view. Therefore, we can state that the exemption does not cover all types of producer groups' income, but only the income closely linked to the essence of the group's and its members' activity.

The third premise relates to the manner and timing of income's disposing to consider it tax-free. The exemption depends on how the income is spent. The exemption concerns only that part of the income, which was spent on behalf of members of APG. Moreover, the Act indicates categories of expenses that enable using the exemption, i.e. the purchase of production's means transferred to group's members,[64] and expenditure on training for group's members. Polish tax authorities claim that the income transfer for the purposes indicated must be definitive and must make it legally possible to fully dispose the object, i.e. it must involve the transfer of the ownership right, not lending or granting the usufruct right.

In the matter of the date limit that entitles to the exemption, the Act requires that the disbursement takes place in the current tax year or the following tax year. Therefore, the later disbursement of the income results in the necessity to tax the income following the general rules[65] due to not meeting the exemption's conditions.

Consequently, we must state that only the cumulative fulfillment of all the conditions mentioned above[66] enables the taxpayer to apply the exemption and show the current tax year's income – in part spent on behalf of the group's members in the current or following tax year – in the statement on the amount of income earned – or loss incurred – as free from CIT.

Moreover, the matter of treating the part of the income spent on behalf of the group's members as tax needs consideration. The disbursement is not always

---

64 It appears from practice that the means is: certified seed, fertilizers, pesticides used or processed during the production cycle, equipment, agricultural machinery. See: individual tax ruling of July 10, 2009, ref. no. ITPB3/432-207/09/DK; individual tax ruling of May 12, 2008, ref. no. IBP3/423-122/08/AK; individual tax ruling of April 11, 2018, ref. no. 0113-KDIPT1-3.4012.6.2018.5.MK; individual tax ruling of April 16, 2018, ref. no. 0113-KDIPT2-1.4011.3.2018.4.AP, www.sip.mf.gov.pl.

65 Art. 7 of the CIT Act.

66 Individual tax ruling of June 12, 2018, ref. no. 0111-KDIB2.4010.115.2018.1.ZK, www.sip.mf.gov.pl.

treated as a dividend payment in a capital company. The construction of the discussed exemption proves that APG is privileged in withdrawing its income in the scope discussed above on behalf of the group's members. The withdrawals are not subject to CIT and are not a share in the legal person's – i.e. APG's – income for the recipients.[67] Therefore, according to tax authorities, the income is not subject to the dividend tax in a situation where the gratuitous profit transfer in the form of means needed for production obtained from the sale of products made and bought in members' holdings, for which the group was registered, and the subsidy granted by ARMA will not take place under a previously adopted resolution of the shareholders' meeting on the distribution of profit. Thus, the transfer will not have the features of a share in the legal persons' profits. The tax authority decided that if only the resolution of the shareholders' meeting accepts the transfer of production means, and it will not be a resolution on profit distribution, the remitter – APG – will not be obliged to collect tax on the share in profits of legal persons.[68] However, as tax authorities indicate, not every benefit – expenditure on the group's members' behalf – is outside the scope of the dividend's concept, and thus is subject to the dividend tax.[69]

Besides, APGs receive financial assistance as support of rural development from the paying agencies and also benefit from tax preferences in this respect. As a rule, the financial aid that APG receives constitutes the group's tax revenue. However, CIT provides for the exemption referred to below.

4. Exemption of Agricultural Cooperatives' and Agricultural Production Cooperatives' Income

We can distinguish two categories in this exemption group. The first category includes the exemption of income of an agricultural cooperative established under the Act on Agricultural Cooperatives.[70] The second category refers to individual incomes of APCs operating on the basis of cooperative law.[71]

67 Individual tax ruling of October 3, 2011, ref. no. IPTPB3/423-107/11-4/IR, www.sip.mf.gov.pl.

68 Individual tax ruling of July 28, 2014, ref. no. IPTPB1/415-253/14-3/KSU; individual tax ruling of February 19, 2014, ref. no. ITPB1/415-1186/13/AD, www.sip.mf.gov.pl.

69 Individual tax ruling of February 4, 2014, ref. no. ITPB3/415-1/13/MK, www.sip.mf.gov.pl.

70 Act of October 4, 2018 on Agricultural Cooperatives (Journal of Laws 2018, item 2073).

71 Act of September 16, 1982 on Cooperative Law Cooperative Law (Journal of Laws 2017, item 1560, as amended), hereinafter: Cooperative Law.

The first category of tax exemption applies to such an agricultural cooperative that operates as a micro-enterprise within the meaning of EU legislation.[72] An agricultural cooperative is a voluntary association of natural or legal persons who: run an agricultural holding or special branches of the agricultural production, are producers of agricultural products or groups of such products, or breed or keep fish, as well as entities who are not farmers, are engaged in the keeping, storage, sorting, packaging or processing of agricultural products, groups of such products or fish produced by farmers or the agricultural supports services, services using machines, tools or equipment for the production of agricultural products, groups of such products or fish by the farmers. A cooperative is an entity with a variable membership and a variable share fund that runs economic activities in the interest of its members. Agricultural cooperatives are to serve the purpose of joint farmers' cooperation in the scope of products made in farmers' holdings or special branches of the agricultural production – including the concentration of supply, marketing, and activities optimizing the costs of production and increasing profitability. Due to the considerably large fragmentation of agricultural holdings in Poland in comparison to the EU, the reasonably large dispersion of supply offered by the holdings is characteristic. At the same time, however, there is a quite dynamic process of consolidation of demand for agricultural products at the level of recipients – agri-food processing, wholesale, and retail trade – in Poland. Agricultural cooperatives are to strengthen the position of common economic structures on the market by farmers. The incentive for promoting such a type of cooperation is the discussed tax exemption. The exemption applies to the income from the sale of agricultural products, groups of such products, or fish, for which the cooperative established, produced in agricultural holdings or special branches of the agricultural production of cooperative's members.[73]

A different legal form of a cooperative character is APCs established on the basis of cooperative law. The object of agricultural production cooperative is to run a joint agricultural holding and actions in the interest of individual agricultural holdings of the members.[74] The cooperative may also run other economic activities or offer its members only specific services. However, the cooperative

72 See: Annex I do the EU Commision's resolution No. 651/2014 of June 17, 2014 declaring certain categories of aid compatible with the internal market in application of articles 107 and 108 of the Treaty (Official Journal of the European Union L 187/1, as amended).

73 See: Art. 17 section 1 point 49a of the CIT Act.

74 Art. 138 of the Cooperative Law.

may also provide its service to non-members and share the resulting profit between cooperative members. The members of the cooperative can be farmers who are: owners or holders of an autonomous agricultural land, leaseholders, users, or other dependent holders of agricultural land. Moreover, other persons with qualifications useful for work in the cooperative may also be members of the cooperative.[75]

The CIT Act provides for a separate exemption for selected agricultural income of APCs. The exemption relates to the income intended for work pay of APSs' members and members of other cooperatives members engaged in agricultural production, and their household members.[76] The exemption is important mainly for the non-agricultural activities or special branches of the agricultural production run by APC in parallel with agricultural activities, as only in such cases the APC's income is determined. The rule does not apply to APCs, which only run agricultural activities as they are not subject to CIT. Thus, if APC runs a non-agricultural economic activity or special branches of agricultural production in parallel, and allocates the non-agricultural income to the remuneration of agricultural cooperative's or other cooperative's members, this income is excluded from CIT.

The basic type of revenue from the membership in an APC is daily wages.[77] Daily wages are part of APG's income attributable to cooperative members.[78] The indicated CIT exemption corresponds to article 33 of the PIT Act.[79] On the basis of the article, APCs and other cooperatives engaged in agricultural production are, as payers, obliged to collect advances on income tax during the year. In this regard, income means: payments made to cooperative members or their household members on account of daily wage, participation in the cooperative's distributed profits, as well as welfares from social insurances obtained by the members.[80]

To sum up, the preference mentioned above has a double legal effect. Effects also refer to the CIT payer in the scope of APG's income. The taxpayer applies

75 Art. 139 of the Cooperative Law.

76 Art. 17 section 1, point 15 of the CIT Act.

77 Individual tax ruling of January 18, 2018, ref. no. 0112-KDIL3-1.4011.335.2017.1.AA, www.sip.mf.gov.pl.

78 The judgment of an Appellate Court in Szczecin of May 25, 2017, ref. no. III AUa 529/16, Legalis; the judgment of the Voivodeship Administrative Court in Gliwice of December 2, 2013, ref. no. I SA/Gl 870/13, CBOSA.

79 Individual tax ruling of February 21, 2011, ref. no. IBPBII/1/415-155/11/AŻ, www.sip.mf.gov.pl.

80 Art. 33 of the PIT Act.

the objective conditional exemption that relates to both non-agricultural and agricultural income – as far as income is not allocated to the remuneration of the cooperative's members and, interestingly enough, their household members. Cooperative members and their household members can work for the cooperative only on the basis of membership. The broad scope of the exemption draws attention. It is so due to the admissibility of employing members of the household besides the members of the cooperative.[81] The work paid with tax-exempt wage must relate to the agricultural activity.[82] Therefore, unlike other categories of taxpayers obtaining income from the non-agricultural activity, remuneration for the work of "employees" is not classified as tax-deductible cost, but is subject to the tax exemption. CIT Act's provisions explain the meaning of such a statutory solution. The CIT Act does not apply to revenue from the agricultural activity, and, therefore, the remuneration related to the activity paid to cooperative members – as an element of tax-deductible costs – is indifferent welfare for the Act.

The legal effects also apply to the status of cooperative as a workplace performing functions of a taxpayer on the basis of CIT. Such a dimension of the preferential position concerning the taxation standard connects with the collection of advance payments for income tax on account of daily wages. The remitter collects such advance payments only from a part of the withdrawals. The part constituting the basis for taxation is determined by such a percentage ratio in which the share of the cooperative's income exempt from CIT in the year preceding the tax year remained – under Art. 17 section 2, point 15 of the CIT Act – in the total amount of payments on account of daily wages. As the judicature emphasizes, the preferential method of calculating advances on PIT does not apply to the prizes paid by a cooperative to its members, as such a provision only applies to withdrawals in respect of the daily wages.[83]

If a cooperative did not generate any income from a non-agricultural activity or special branches of agricultural production in the previous year, no tax advances ought to be deducted from the current withdrawals on account of daily

81 According to Art. 156 of the Cooperative Law, a member of the cooperative's member family is considered a household member, as well as other persons living together and running a household with the cooperative member.

82 The judgment of the Supreme Administrative Court in Katowice of September 15, 1997, ref. no. I SA/Ka 329/96, CBOSA.

83 The judgment of the Supreme Administrative Court of May 13, 2016, ref. no. II FSK 923/14, CBOSA.

wages for cooperative members and their household members.[84] APGs and other cooperatives engaged in agricultural production are obliged to separate income and costs relating to agricultural plant and animal production not subject to special branches of agricultural production in their accounting records. Compliance with such a statutory requirement should make it easier for taxpayers to determine the share of exempt income in the total income earned by a taxpayer.

5. Other objective exemptions

The other objective exemptions, which are in practice important for legal persons conducting an agricultural activity, as well as special branches of agricultural production or mixed activities, should include the exemption of direct subsidies applied under CAP of the European Union. Subsidies are received on the basis of separate provisions.[85] Exemptions should as well include amounts received from government agencies or executive agencies if the agencies have received funds for this purpose from the state budget, except for subsidies for the interest rate on bank loans to the extent specified in separate acts.[86] Due to this study's character, we only concentrate on problems raised by the indicated taxpayers' categories.

The first of the mentioned exemptions relates to direct subsidies applied under the EU's CAP. Currently, the European Parliament's and Council's resolution of 2013 regulates the direct subsidies system in the EU.[87] Subsidies cover farmers defined in the up-mentioned act as natural or legal persons, or groups of natural or legal persons, regardless of the legal status of such a group and its members under the national law, whose farm is in the EU and who pursue an agricultural activity.[88] Categories of direct subsidies are not permanent in nature and change.[89]

---

84 Individual tax ruling of January 18, 2018, ref. no. 0112-KDIL3-1.4011.335.2017.1.AA, www.sip.mf.gov.pl.

85 Art. 17 section 1, point 36 of the CIT Act.

86 Art. 17 section 1, point 48 of the CIT Act.

87 Regulation (EU) No. 1307/2013 of the European Parliament and of the Council of of December 17, 2013 establishing rules for direct subsidies to farmers under support schemes within the framework of the common agricultural policy and repealing Council Regulation (EC) No. 637/2008 and Council Regulation (EC) No. 73/2009 (Official Journal of the European Union L 347/608 as amended). Further: Regulation No 1307/2013.

88 Art. 4 section 1, regulation No. 1307/2013.

89 Under national law, the Act of February 5, 2015 on subsidies under direct support schemes (Journal of Laws 2018, item 1312 as amended), together with several executive acts, which implement the principles set out in EU law, is in force.

It is clear from the case-law that the exemption in question does not cover export refunds, which we cannot regard as direct subsidies under the mentioned provisions.[90] However, export refunds are subject to a separate exemption under Art. 18 section 1, point 48 of the CIT Act.

The exemption of subsidies under the EU's CAP with separate tax relief. According to Art. 17 section 1, point 36a, claims, and debts owed to paying agencies under the agricultural policy, as well as claims relating to unduly or excessively collected payments under direct support schemes and under rural development support with contributions from the European Agricultural Fund for Rural Development, which were waived, are also exempt from CIT. The new exemption was added by an amendment to the law on support for rural development with contributions from the European Agricultural Fund for Rural Development.[91] Therefore the exemption is used for dues remitted to agricultural producer entities. Executive acts govern the detailed rules for remitting, postponing, or arranging installments of the payment of debts owed to the paying agencies under CAP.[92] The president of the paying agency, i.e. AMRA, ex officio remits dues from the funds set in the regulation as long as the amount receivable does not exceed the equivalent of 100.00 euro.

The second exemption concerns quotas received from government agencies or executive agencies if they received funds from the state budget for such a purpose, except for interest rate subsidies on bank loans. Government agencies, which are part of the public finance sector,[93] are state legal persons created by separate acts to perform public tasks. The tasks of the agency, apart from managing the property of the State Treasury and performing tasks on behalf of the state, also include supporting selected types of economic activity. For such a reason, agencies often receive funds from the state budget for a specific purpose and mediate in transferring the funds to other entities. The exemption in

---

90 The judgment of the Supreme Administrative Court of February 8, 2011, ref. no. II FSK 1779/09, CBOSA; the judgment of the Supreme Administrative Court of May 18, 2010, ref. no. II FSK 31/09, CBOSA.

91 Act of July 28, 2011 on amending the Act on supporting rural development with the funds from the European Agricultural Fund for Rural Development and on amending certain other acts (Journal of Laws 2011, item 1202).

92 Resolution of the Council of Ministers of December 21, 2010 on detailed rules and procedures for remitting, postponing, or arranging installments of receivables due to paying agencies under CAP (Journal of Laws 2010, No. 258, item 1747 as amended).

93 Art. 9, point 14 of the Act of August 27, 2009 on Public Finance (Journal of Laws 2019, item 869 as amended).

question concerns income from such a source and is a logical complement to the exemption expressed in Art. 17 section 1, point 47. The exemption also contains the same limitation of application to interest rate subsidies on bank loans, to the extent laid down in separate laws. However, the exemption does not cover quotas which the taxpayer receives from other funds at the disposal of the agencies, including budgetary subsidies for agencies' operation. The provision refers only to quotas which are transferred to an agency and which already were earmarked for a specific purpose when they are transferred from the State budget. The provision refers only to quotas that are transferred with agencies' intermediation and which already were earmarked for a specific purpose while transferring from the state budget.

In practice, in the field of agriculture, the problem of exemption for export refunds arose. Export refunds are applied in the framework of the EU's CAP to ensure the adequate competitiveness of agri-food products produced in the European Union. The current EU act governing the possibility of granting such refunds is Regulation (EU) No. 1308/2013 of the European Parliament and of the Council establishing a common organization of markets in agricultural products.[94] The act defines the scope and rules of application of export refunds. To the extent necessary to enable exports on the basis of world market quotations or prices and within limits resulting from international agreements, the difference between those prices and prices in the Union may be covered by export refunds for products of certain sectors exported without further processing. Refunds are granted in the following sectors: cereals; rice; sugar, beef and veal; milk and milk products; pig meat; eggs; poultry meat; including exports in the form of goods processed under European Union law.

Polish judicial decisions unequivocally recognized that export refunds obtained by the taxpayer use the exemption regulated in Art. 17 section 1, point 48 of the Act.[95] The consequence of applying the exemption in question is the necessity to exclude the expenses and costs directly financed from income (revenue) from tax-deductible costs.[96] Expenses and costs directly financed from

94 Regulation (EU) No. 1308/2013 of the European Parliament and of the Council of 12.17.2013 establishing a common organization of markets of agricultural products and repealing Council Regulations (EEC) No 922/72, (EEC) No 234/79, (EC) No 1037/2001 and (EC) No 1234/2007 (Official Journal of the European Union L347/671 as amended).

95 The judgment of the Voivodeship Administrative Court in Poznań of October 3, 2013, ref. no. I SA/Po 258/13; the judgment of the Voivodeship Administrative Court in Wrocław of June 17, 2016, ref. no. I SA/Wr 301/16, CBOSA.

96 See: Art. 16 section 1, point 58 of the CIT Act.

the income (revenue) covered by the exemption in question are not regarded as tax-deductible.

V. Final remarks

The taxation of the agricultural and mixed – i.e. agricultural-related – activity in Poland has an archaic structure. The structure did not change significantly since the post-war period. The current model of taxation of legal persons and organizational units conducting agricultural and mixed activity bases on a preferential exclusion of agricultural activity from the income tax and its coverage by the agricultural tax. Therefore, such a model bases on taxation of the territorial norm with simultaneous resignation from determining income from the activity in question.

The taxation of special branches of the agricultural production with CIT does not differ from the standard taxation rules of other entrepreneurs. On the other hand, the legal structure of tax exemptions indicates quite considerable tax privileges for such CIT payers operating in the agricultural sector. It is not only about the subjective exemptions but also about the possibility of using preferences in activity concentration, e.g. in the form of a tax capital group, agricultural cooperatives, or agricultural producer groups.

The analysis of judicial decisions and the position of tax authorities, apart from a wide range of tax problems faced by Polish CIT payers in the area of tax law application, also gives a picture of indicated entities functioning on the basis of the full professionalism. The analysis also allows noticing the multifaceted organizational and factual possibilities within the scope of activity that do not deviate from the standard taxed entities without tax privileges, often conducting a business activity or special branches of agricultural production in identical legal forms, i.e. companies.

The argumentation justifying the "tax preference system's" functioning addressed to legal persons conducting an agricultural and mixed activity introduced since the 1990s until the pre-accession period is no longer valid. The changes that took place in recent years, and in particular the inclusion of persons conducting the agricultural activity in the EU's CAP, significantly strengthened their legal and economic situation. It seems that the current special privileges of the group of taxpayers in question on the grounds of CIT are not justified and require legislative changes. However, the changes, in the case of the category of agricultural entrepreneurs in question, will not be revolutionary, as should be the case with farmers who are natural persons. The concept of sectoral equality should be considered when developing a new taxation model for agricultural entrepreneurs that are natural persons as well as legal persons and unincorporated entities. On the other hand, however, a uniform, non-privileged taxation standard should be introduced as part of the corporate tax structure, regardless of the type of activity carried out by taxpayers.

Chapter Four: Taxation of the Agricultural Land

I. General remarks

The agricultural tax stands out from other public levies in the Polish tax system. First of all, the Agricultural Tax Act is in force for one of the most extended periods. Moreover, the Act was introduced in entirely different social, economic, and political conditions than those existing today, i.e. specific to the free market economy. It was the period of the centrally planned economy, characteristic for the communist totalitarian systems of the then Eastern European countries. Although at the beginning of the 1990s there was a significant change in the statutory regulation concerning the taxation of specialized agricultural activities as a result of the income tax reform, the underlying assumptions of the agricultural land taxation maintained a similar outline to the present day. Noteworthy, until the moment of introducing the change, the agricultural tax was the only tax burdening agricultural activity in Poland. The tax covered both usual and specialized agricultural activity. As a result of legislative changes, the operation consisting in conventional agricultural production – i.e. cultivation of agricultural land – was subject to the agricultural tax, while specialist, highly profitable agricultural production – e.g. breeding fur animals, production in greenhouses and mushroom farms – was subject to income taxes. Thus, the agricultural tax became a taxation form of the holding and other agricultural lands.

II. Taxpayers

The Agricultural Tax Act does not specify a particular category of a farmer-taxpayer. Taxpayers are natural persons, legal persons, and organizational units without the legal personality, which are possessors of land, autonomous possessors, perpetual usufructuaries, or holders of the land owned by the State Treasury or local government units. In principle, in the case of land owned by the State Treasury or local government units, holding must result from an agreement. Exceptionally, the Act allows such holding to occur also without a legal title. In the case of land that is part of the Agricultural Property Stock of the State Treasury or is managed by the State Forests, the organizational units of the National Center for Agricultural Support and the State Forests are the agricultural tax payers. The State Treasury and communes exclude from taxation.

In practice, there are difficulties in taxing autonomous possessors. In such a case, there are two entities: the autonomous possessor and the owner of the agricultural land. According to the Act, the autonomous possessor is liable to the tax. However, a decision imposing the tax may address the autonomous possessor only if the tax authority establishes that the real estate is in the autonomous possession of a person other than the owner. In such a case, the tax authority should run an appropriate investigation to identify the autonomous possessor. It is essential to identify the possessor as the land, and the building register does not always show the holder of the land and buildings.

The Agricultural Tax Act provides that, in strictly defined situations, a dependent owner may act like a taxpayer, i.e. when the land on which the agricultural production is carried out is leased. First, such a situation occurs when the territory of an agricultural holding was leased in whole or in part on the basis of a contract concluded under the provisions on social insurance of farmers or the regulations on obtaining a structural pension.[1] According to the Act, the land should be leased on the basis of a written agreement concluded for at least ten years, and notified to the Land and Property Register. The land may not be leased to the pensioner's spouse, pensioner's descendants or stepchildren and their spouses, and persons and their spouses remaining in the common household with the pensioner. The second case concerns contracts on farm transfers concluded under the Structural Pensions Act.[2] The case includes land forming part of a holding transferred to enlarge one or more existing holdings. The legislator made it an additional condition that the area of the enlarged holding may not be less than 15 ha. Also, the agreement mentioned above may be concluded with a natural person who fulfills all of the following conditions: is a farmer, has agricultural qualifications, has no established right to a pension from social security or pension provision. The regulations allow the possibility of concluding a contract with a legal person, provided that the scope of such an entity's activity includes an agricultural activity.

Moreover, we should point out that, in the case of an agricultural holding land contributed to a production cooperative, it is the production cooperative that will be liable to pay the agricultural tax, and not lands' owner.

If two or more entities own a land classified in the Land and Property Register as agricultural land, it should be taxed separately. The co-owners or holders

1 Art. 3 section 3 of the Agricultural Tax Act.

2 Act of April 26, 2001 on the Structural Pensions (Journal of Laws 2001, No. 52, item 539 as amended).

should be jointly and severally liable for payment. The discussed regulations do not apply in a situation where land constitutes an agricultural holding. In such a case, the person who runs an agricultural holding in its entirety bears the tax obligation.[3] However, the Act does not define the concept of "running an agricultural holding in its entirety," which in practice causes numerous difficulties in interpretation.

III. Subject of taxation

The land which is registered as an agricultural land in the Land and Property Register is subject to agricultural tax. Besides, the area may not be occupied for activities other than agricultural activities.

The Agricultural Tax Act does not define the term "agricultural land." Therefore, the regulation of the Minister of Regional Development and Construction on the registration of land and buildings is used to determine the term.[4] The literature rightly emphasizes that the situation provokes controversy in terms of constitutional standards. In the current state of affairs, not an act, but a regulation of the Minister determines the form of the tax.[5]

There are nine categories of agricultural land. These are:

1) **arable lands**, which the land register marks with the symbol – R. The RLB Act defines such an area as being under permanent mechanical cultivation for agricultural or horticultural production; suitable for mechanical cultivation but occupied under hop, wicker or ornamental tree plantations, including hemlock firs, and nurseries for ornamental trees or shrubs, or on which family allotment gardens were arranged; occupied under facilities and structures supporting agricultural or horticultural production and located outside the habitat parcel; maintained as fallow or set aside;
2) **permanent grasslands**, marked with the symbol – Ł, include: land covered with dense perennial vegetation which consists of numerous species of grasses, papilionaceous plants, and herbs, thus creating systematically

3 See: Art. 3 section 5 and 6 of the Agricultural Tax Act.

4 Regulation of the Minister of Regional Development and Construction of March 29, 2001 on the registration of land and buildings (Journal of Laws 2016, item 1034 as amended), hereinafter: RLB Act.

5 M. Burzec, "Podatek rolny," in: *Opodatkowanie rolnictwa w Polsce…*, p. 359.

mown meadow sward, and in mountain areas – pastures and halves, usually harvested;

3) **permanent pastures**, marked with the symbol – Ps, locate on a land with similar vegetation to the grassland on which the livestock grazes and, in mountain areas, mountain pastures and meadows which, as a rule, are not mown but on which the livestock grazes, including land occupied for livestock support facilities such as shelters and coops for the animals, located outside the habitat parcel;
4) **orchards**, marked with the symbol – S, include: land of at least 0,10 ha on which fruit trees or fruit shrubs grow in a compact planting (minimum 600 trees or 2000 shrubs per ha), or on which fruit tree or shrub nurseries or vineyards were established;
5) **pond bottoms**, marked with the symbol – Wsr, under the regulation on land and property registration are lands under water bodies equipped with hydrotechnical devices, suitable for fish farming, breeding, and keeping. Such areas include fenced-in areas with a system of ditches and areas adjacent and associated with ponds belonging to a pond. The land with the symbol Wsr is the land under lakes and dam reservoirs with technical devices for water level regulation;
6) **built-up agricultural land**, marked with the symbol – Br, includes, among other things: area occupied for housing and other buildings and installations,[6] buildings intended for agricultural production[7] including fish production, and buildings designed for agri-food processing – excluding land occupied for industrial agricultural processing plants using raw materials from outside the agricultural holding of which the buildings are part;

6 Annex No. 6 of the RLB Act lists the following buildings and construction equipment: boiler rooms, cells, garages, sheds, shelters, granaries, livestock buildings, storage and maneuvering yards within the building area.

7 Such as: granaries, fruit and vegetable warehouses, barns, livestock buildings, buildings for agricultural equipment, fish warehouses and sorting plants, fish hatcheries, fish farms, smokehouses, processing plants, cold stores, as well as agricultural buildings and equipment, in particular: liquid manure tanks, manure storage slabs, silage silos, grain and fodder silos, fermentation chambers and agricultural biogas tanks, as well as installations for the production of agricultural biogas, storage yards, parking and maneuvering areas for agricultural machinery.

7) **ditches bottoms**, marked with the – W symbol, include: land occupied by open ditches which serve as water drainage facilities for the area used for agricultural production;
8) **wooded and bushed land on agricultural land**, marked with the symbol – Lzr, include: an area that is enclaves or semi-enclaves of agricultural land on which there are mid-field clusters of trees and shrubs or only trees aged over ten years and not classified as forest or orchards;
9) **wastelands**, marked with the symbol – N, are agricultural land which is not suitable for agricultural production activities without significant inputs (e.g. sands, marshes, natural physiographic works in the form of cliffs, rocks, rubble).

It is worth underscoring that this list of land subject to the agricultural tax is closed. In principle, the area which does not constitute agricultural land is subject to real estate tax or forestry tax. Unfortunately, in practice, there are problems with proper classification resulting from outdated information in the Land and Property Register. Unreliable data in the register causes that the tax liability may be established improperly. The more so, because the tax authorities, as a rule, are bound by the data contained in the register.[8] Such a situation often happens also because taxpayers only want to update the land data if the update has any impact on reducing the tax burden. The impossibility for the tax authority to apply for updating the data contained in the Land and Property Register is an obvious disadvantage of the existing system.

---

8 The judgment of the Supreme Administrative Court of November 29, 2015, ref. no. II FSK 2027/13, CBOSA; the judgment of the Supreme Administrative Court of January 13, 2015, ref. no. II FSK 3108/12, CBOSA; the judgment of the Voivodeship Administrative Court in Gliwice of September 20, 2016, ref. no. I SA/Gl 1242/15, CBOSA; the judgment of the Voivodeship Administrative Court in Bydgoszcz of October 28, 2015, ref. no. I SA/Bd 686/15, CBOSA; the judgment of the Voivodeship Administrative Court in Lublin of October 26, 2011, ref. no. I SA/Lu 500/11, CBOSA. See also: B. Pahl, Gloss to the judgment of the Voivodeship Administrative Court in Gdańsk of March 15, 2006, ref. no. I SA/Gd 348/04 on land and property registration as a basis for local taxes, *Przegląd Podatków Lokalnych i Finansów Samorządowych*, No. 5, (2009), pp. 1 and 4. Recently, there were tendencies in the case law to question the data contained in the Land and Property Register. For more on this subject, see: K. Radzikowski, "Odrzucenie danych z ewidencji gruntów i budynków na potrzeby wymiaru podatków lokalnych w świetle najnowszego orzecznictwa sądów administracyjnych," *Samorząd Terytorialny* No. 4, (2016), pp. 70 ff.

As already indicated, land cannot be occupied for economic activities other than agricultural activities for the purposes of agricultural tax. The area on which economic activity is pursued should be exempted from the agricultural tax.[9] However, in light of the jurisdiction, the term "seizure of land for the purpose of conducting economic activity" means that not only physical intervention in the ground but also actions of a legal nature that fall within the scope of the economic activity.[10] Moreover, in Polish tax law, in the context of land taxation, the term "engaged in" is similar to the term "connected with" economic activity. The legislator uses the term in the construction of real estate tax regulated by the Local Taxes and Fees Act. We should understand the land "connected with" running an economic activity as an area in the entrepreneur's possession. The court-administrative decisions indicate a wide range of the statutory meaning of the term "connected with." It is argued that land connected with running an economic activity is not always perceived as occupied for running such an activity. However, in each case, the area occupied for economic activity will be associated with such an activity by definition.[11] It is so since the term "connected with" the conducted economic activity includes not only the actual running of specific activity on a given property but also estate's possession by entities having the status of entrepreneurs.

The **concept of agricultural activity** is an essential issue in this context. The Agricultural Tax Act defined agricultural activity as plant and animal production including the production of seed, nursery, breeding and reproduction material, vegetable production, ornamental plants, mushrooms production, horticulture,

---

9 See, among other things: the judgment of the Voivodeship Administrative Court in Cracow of July 10, 2017, ref. no. I SA/Kr 1435/16, CBOSA; the judgment of the Voivodeship Administrative Court in Warsaw of April 10, 2015, ref. no. III SA/Wa 2663/14, CBOSA; See also: L. Etel, *Podatek rolny. Podatek leśny. Komentarz* (Warsaw, 2012), pp. 37–39; P. Borszowski, K. Stelmaszczyk, *Podatki i opłaty lokalne. Podatek rolny. Podatek leśny. Komentarz* (Warsaw, 2016), pp. 374–379.

10 See: the judgment of the Supreme Administrative Court of May 14, 2015, ref. no. II FSK 190/15, CBOSA; the judgment of the Voivodeship Administrative Court in Szczecin of July 26, 2017, ref. no. I SA/Sz 431/17, CBOSA; the judgment of the Voivodeship Administrative Court in Gdańsk of April 11, 2017, ref. no. I SA/Gd 170/17, CBOSA.

11 See: the judgment of the Voivodeship Administrative Court in Warsaw of February 26, 2013, ref. no. III SA/Wa 3242/12, CBOSA; the judgment of the Voivodeship Administrative Court in Wrocław of January 25, 2013, ref. no. I SA/Wr 1364/12, CBOSA; the judgment of the Voivodeship Administrative Court in Warsaw of September 21, 2011, ref. no. III SA/Wa 120/11, CBOSA.

husbandry and production of germ material of animals, fowl and commercial insects, animal production of industrial and farm type, as well as fish farming. Any other activity not falling under the above definition is not an agricultural activity. Therefore, if it is carried out on agricultural land, such land should not be subject to agricultural tax.

We have already discussed the problem of agricultural activity definition in the Polish legal order in the earlier part of this monograph. At this point, it is only necessary to mark the controversies and legal barriers that emerge in practice. As already mentioned, there are two definitions of agricultural activity in the Polish tax system. One definition bases on the grounds of the Agricultural Tax Act and the other one bases on Income Tax Acts. The definition of an agricultural activity included in income taxes is not the same as the definition which appears in the agricultural tax law. Noteworthy, while the CIT Act defines the agricultural activity as an activity consisting in keeping purchased animals and plants in normatively defined minimum periods, the Agricultural Tax Act misses similar solutions. In such a case, the activity consisting in keeping purchased animals and plants, on the one hand, is considered an agricultural activity – under Acts on Income Taxes – and, on the other hand, is not – see: Agricultural Tax Act. According to the current provisions of law, keeping animals and plants exclude from taxation in income taxes, while at the same time, it was not indicated in the definition of an agricultural activity contained in the Agricultural Tax Act.[12] Therefore, if the activity in question happens in the area classified in the Land and Property Register as agricultural land, then doubts may arise whether such an area should be subject to the agricultural tax in relation to specific activities undertaken by the taxpayer. It seems justified to demand to formulate a uniform definition of agricultural activity for tax purposes.

In the current design of the agricultural tax, it is crucial to determine whether the land is a **part of an agricultural holding**. Such an action affects the determination of the appropriate tax base and the application of the proper tax rate. For tax purposes, the term agricultural holding is: "the area of usable agricultural land, and wooded and planted area on the usable agricultural land, with a total area exceeding 1 ha or 1 conversion ha, owned or held by a natural person, legal entity, or organizational unit, including a company without legal personality." The definition adopted on the basis of the tax law provisions refers to meeting the area standard of the land adequately classified in the Land and Property

12 Art. 2 section 1, point 1 of the PIT Act and Art. 2 section 2 of the CIT Act.

Register. The only criterion for recognizing land as an agricultural holding is its total area. It is not essential whether agricultural land creates an economic bond with another agricultural land. Parts of land located on the territory of Poland in two distant locations may be recognized as an agricultural holding if the total area exceeds 1 ha or 1 conversion ha.

Noteworthy, there are two definitions of an agricultural holding in the Polish legal system. One definition bases on civil law, the other on tax law. According to the Civil Code, an agricultural holding is: "an agricultural land together with forest land, buildings or buildings' parts, equipment and inventory, if it constitutes or may constitute an organized economic whole, that has rights and obligations related to running an agricultural holding."[13] Therefore, the civil law definition is much broader than the definition adopted for tax purposes. In constructing the tax definition, the functional approach was abandoned. From a practical point of view, such a concept is correct. The use of the operational definition of an agricultural holding in the Civil Code would lead to numerous disputes. Contrary to the civil law, in the tax law, land constituting an agricultural holding does not have to form an organized whole.[14]

In assessing the up-mentioned solution, it seems that the current definition of an agricultural holding is defective, especially when rightly assuming that the purpose of economic activity is to achieve a specific objective. Most often, the goal is the financial result in the form of revenue or income. In fact, agricultural activity is a form of conducting economic activity, even though the Polish Act on the Law of Entrepreneurs excludes its application to production activity in agriculture in the field of crop production, animal keeping and breeding, horticulture, vegetable farming, forestry, and inland fishing.[15] The aim of an agricultural holding in the free market economy is to produce plant and animal products. However, the solutions adopted by the legislator may suggest that an agricultural holding is not a means to achieve the objective of profit-oriented agricultural production.

In fact, recognizing an agricultural holding on the basis of the area standard is questionable. Such a recognition results in a higher tax burden on those lands whose area is less than 1 ha or 1 conversion ha. In practice, some types of plant or

13 Art. 55 [3] of the Civil Code.

14 See: G. Liszewski, "Reforma podatku rolnego – próba oceny," in: *Polski system podatkowy. Założenia a praktyka*, ed. A. Pomorska (Lublin, 2004), pp. 334–336.

15 Art. 6 section 1, point 1 of the Act of March 6, 2018 on the Entrepreneurs Law (Journal of Laws 2019, item 1292).

animal production do not always require a large area of land, for example, trout farming or running an apiary. Thus, on the one hand, the activity consisting in production or breeding on an area of less than 1 ha or 1 conversion ha will be considered an agricultural activity. On the other hand, within the meaning of the Agricultural Tax Act, such a type of activity will not be run within the agricultural holding, as the area standard condition will not be met. Therefore, in light of provisions currently in force, a situation may occur in which an entity conducting an agricultural activity on a land with an area of less than 1 ha or 1 conversion ha will be charged a higher agricultural tax than an entity having nothing to do with agricultural production but owning land which is part of an agricultural holding – i.e. exceeding the indicated area standard.

IV. Tax preferences

The agricultural tax is a tribute with relatively low fiscal efficiency. Compared to other taxes, the agricultural tax is generally not an efficient source of the budgetary revenue. At the same time, the Agricultural Tax Act contains a relatively extensive list of various tax preferences. We can divide the preferences into two basic groups:

a) tax exemptions
b) tax reliefs

The wide range of **exemptions** contained in the construction of the agricultural tax results from the specific nature of the levy in question. In such a context, we can distinguish three groups of exemptions. The first one is the subjective exemptions; it concerns entities that do not run an agricultural production but only possess the area classified in the Land and Property Register as usable agricultural land. Noteworthy, entities exempted from the agricultural tax on land use the same tax advantage also in the real estate tax and forestry tax. The taxpayers exempt from the agricultural tax are, as follows: universities; science institutes and auxiliary science units of the Polish Academy of Sciences; research and development units; the National Real Estate Stock; public and non-public organizational units covered by the education system and the bodies running them – in the scope of land occupied for educational activities; entities running supported employment enterprises; entrepreneurs with the status of research and development centers.

The second group of exemptions refers to the land that cannot be freely owned. It is due to the specific nature of the area in question for the public or land's physical characteristics, which make it practically impossible to use the land under the will of the holder. The exemption covers following types of area: land under dikes and land situated in between dikes; land situated in the strip of a border road; usable ecological land; land entered in the register of historical monuments, provided that it is managed and maintained under the legislation on the protection and care of historical monuments; area occupied by water bodies.

The third group of exemptions relates to the land used principally for agricultural production, in the case when, for specific reasons, the area is not profitable as it cannot be used for agricultural activities (wholly or partly). The Agricultural Tax Act exempts for the above reasons: land subject to drainage; land on which the agricultural production has ceased; land of classes V, VI, and VIz; land obtained by exchange or consolidation. Also, in the agricultural tax, there is an exemption of farmland formed from a wasteland, and an exemption of land intended for the creation of a new farm or extension of an existing one to an area not exceeding 100 ha. Such regulations' existence results from an outdated construction of the agricultural tax.

The group of exemptions in question, contained in the Agricultural Tax Act, is of closed character. Nevertheless, the Agricultural Tax Act provides for the possibility of introducing other exemptions of a subjective nature by a resolution of the commune council. Administrative boundaries of a particular commune delimit the territorial scope of the exemptions granted in such a way.

The broad scope of the envisaged exemptions and the adopted framework of this study lead to the abandonment of a detailed discussion of all tax exemptions. However, it is worth noting more attention to a few selected exemptions concerning land related to agricultural production.

The **exemption relating to agricultural land of classes V, VI, and VIz** raises numerous controversies.[16] The purpose of introducing the preference mentioned above was to support the processes of agricultural land utilization, as well as to consider investment costs for such a type of land.[17] However, such an exemption to which no territorial restriction was applied, depletes the budget revenues of communes. Such a situation results from the fact that in the territory of Poland, the quality structure of soils used for crops is unfavorable. In practice, the most fertile soils, such as rendzinas, black soils, alluvial soils, and chernozems, account for only 9 % of the total land area. Brown soils and podzolic soils that are of medium fertility cover nearly ¾ of the country's area. On the territory of the

16 Art. 12 section 1, point 1 of the Agricultural Tax Act.

17 A. Hanusz, *Polityka podatkowa w zakresie różnicowania obciążeń dochodów rolniczych w Polsce* (Lublin, 1996), pp. 228–231.

whole of Poland, the land classified in the I class constitutes only 0.36 % of all land, while in the II class – 2.89 %.[18] Since Poland does not have good conditions for field crops, the exemption from taxation of the agricultural land classified in class V raises many doubts. Such a land constitutes about 22.64 % of the total area of cultivated land in Poland.[19] Although such lands classify as weak land, they can be used to grow rye, lupine, sometimes potatoes, or even some fruit tree crops. The use of such a type of agricultural land depends primarily on the hydrographic conditions and the degree of cultivation. In communes where both the degree of cultivation and the hydrological conditions are good, such land should not be exempt from taxation. It seems that in the case of class V land, the agricultural tax exemption should be a preference of territorial scope. In this case, the degree of cultivation and hydrographic conditions should be considered, as well as the land quality in a given commune. Such an exemption should be granted by way of a resolution of the commune council in a commune where the usable agricultural land in question is located. It would be justifiable for the commune council to grant an exemption from agricultural tax on class V usable agricultural land in the case where the commune is located on good or very good soils. However, from a fiscal point of view, a statutory exemption, such as is currently the case for class V usable agricultural land situated in comunes where 50 % of the area is land of such a class, is not justified.

The same applies to usable agricultural land of classes VI and VIz. A controversial issue is the possibility of tax exemption for the usable agricultural land not included in the agricultural holding. Such a situation is inconsistent with the legislator, as the purpose of the exemption is to support the processes of the usable agricultural land utilization and to consider investment costs for such a type of land. We know that such processes closely relate to agricultural production. Meanwhile, entities that actually have nothing in common with the agricultural production may benefit from the exemption. Such a situation is particularly the case in suburban communes, where often single-family house estates are built on usable agricultural land. It seems incomprehensible, primarily since the Agricultural Tax Act defines the concept of agricultural activity. Therefore, changes should be introduced to limit the scope of the exemption. First, only classes V, VI, and VI of agricultural land belonging to agricultural

18 See: *Rocznik Statystyczny. Rolnictwo 2009*, ed. M. Osiński (Warsaw, 2009), p. 75.

19 *Rocznik*. . ., ed. M. Osiński, p. 75. Additionally, the IV class land, which accounts for 37.24 % of the total land use, is the most numerous in Poland, while the III class land accounts for 31.81 %.

holdings should exempt from the tax. Second, the exemption from agricultural tax on class V usable agricultural land should be optional and apply if the commune council adopts an appropriate resolution in this respect. Third, it should be considered whether granting the exemption in question should not take place only concerning those entities which carry out an agricultural activity.

Land of agricultural holdings where agricultural production ceased is also exempt from the agricultural tax. Such a preference limits to 20 % of the usable agricultural land of the holding, but not more than 10 ha. Moreover, the exemption in question is granted to taxpayers for a period not longer than three years. However, we do not know which usable agricultural land the taxpayer can present for the exemption. As a rule, the taxpayer will indicate the best class land as this will lead to the reduction of the tax burden. The wording referring to the exemption lasting not longer than three years concerning the same area may be challenging to interpret. The literal formula of the law indicates a time limit which cannot be longer than three years. We should consider the term stated in the Act as the total period during which the preference in question applies to the same land. Thus, in relation to the same area, the exemption may be used once for the whole period indicated in the Act, or several times in shorter periods, which, when added together, may not exceed three years. The exemption is granted by decision at the request of the taxpayer. A resolution of individual commune councils should determine the procedure and conditions of an explicit exemption. Failure to adopt a relevant resolution by a commune council does not give rise to any grounds to refuse to apply the exemption in question. The reason for this is the position expressed by the Supreme Administrative Court, according to which the consequences of negligence and irregularities committed by the legislator cannot pass on to taxpayers.[20] Moreover, a resolution of the commune council cannot narrow the scope of the exemption in question granted under the Agricultural Tax Act.[21]

The Agricultural Tax Act contains two exemptions of a stimulative nature. The first one is **the exemption of agricultural holding land created from developing wastelands**. The preference mentioned above covers the period of 5 years counting from the year following the completion of the development.[22]

20 The judgment of the Supreme Administrative Court of May 14, 1993, ref. no. III SA 2231/92, CBOSA.

21 The judgment of the Supreme Administrative Court of April 4, 1993, ref. no. SA/Wr 1449/92, CBOSA.

22 Art. 12 section 1, point 5 of the Agricultral Tax Act. After the expiry of the exemption period, the Act provides for applying an agricultural tax relief consisting of a 75 % reduction in the first year and 50 % in the second year.

Unfortunately, the provisions of the Agricultural Tax Act do not specify the term "development," which leads to numerous difficulties in interpretation. Additionally, the notion of "wasteland" is also questionable as there is no definition of "wasteland" in the Agricultural Tax Act. The exemption mentioned above is granted at the request of the taxpayer by way of a decision of the head of a commune, mayor, or town president. The legislator introduced the initial moment of using the exemption, which is the year following the year in which the development ended.

The second stimulative exemption concerns land intended for the establishment of a new agricultural holding or the extension of an existing one to an area not exceeding 100 ha.[23] The exemption is temporary in nature. It is granted at the request of the taxpayer by a decision of the head of a commune, mayor or town president for a period of 5 years, counting from the first day of the month following the month in which the agreement on the sale of land or perpetual usufruct rights was concluded, the right of perpetual usufruct of land was established, or the land was included in permanent usage.[24] If a taxpayer acquires or obtains land with an area of less than 100 ha, then the exemption applies to the land successively purchased or obtained for permanent usage. In such a case, the exemption limits to the total area not exceeding 100 ha. In connection with land acquisition or obtaining it on the basis of several legal acts, the exemption period determines separately. The provisions of the Agricultural Tax Act do not allow for the possibility of exemption from taxation if the land which was previously taken by the purchaser in permanent usage was acquired through the sale from the Agricultural Property Stock of the State Treasury. The Agricultural Tax Act also excludes the possibility to take advantage of the exemption in the case of purchasing land from individual owners of agricultural holdings if the purchaser is a spouse, a related person, or an affinity of the land seller.[25]

The purpose of the preference in question is to encourage people with agricultural holdings to intensify agricultural production. The intensification supposed to happen due to increasing the area of land on which agricultural activity takes place. However, the regulations mentioned above are questionable. The

---

23 Art. 12 section 1, point 4 of the Agricultural Tax Act.

24 Art. 12 section 3 of the Agricultral Tax Act. After the expiry of the exemption period, the Act provides for applying an agricultural tax relief consisting of a 75 % reduction in the first year and 50 % in the second year.

25 Pursuant to Art. 12 section 5 of the Agricultural Tax Act, the purchaser cannot be a spouse, relative in a straight line or his spouse, stepson, son-in-law or daughter-in-law of a land seller.

provisions of the Agricultural Tax Act introduce several conditions which must be met for agricultural land intended for the establishment of a new agricultural holding or the extension of an existing one to benefit from a temporary agricultural tax exemption:

1) the limit of the area of the newly created or enlarged agricultural holding;
2) the form of obtaining the land legally;
3) the purpose of acquiring or obtaining the land for permanent usage.

One of the premises for taking advantage of the exemption in question is the creation of a new agricultural holding or the extension of an existing one to an area not exceeding 100 ha. In the resolution of October 20, 1997, the Supreme Administrative Court took the position[26] that applying the exemption should be excluded in the case of establishment or enlargement of an agricultural holding if its area exceeds 100 ha.[27] The Court stressed that the provision introducing the exemption does not contain any settlements that would provide for exempting part of the taken land from the agricultural tax with simultaneous taxation of the land surplus. Incidentally, we should emphasize that the provision introducing the exemption also does not contain any specific settlements excluding such a possibility. However, according to the Court, the lack of an explicit indication in this regard suggests that the legislative authorities did not allow such an option. The provisions regulating exempting agricultural land on which agricultural production ceased, and which indicate what percentage of the area may be exempt confirm the thesis above.[28] Regarding the above, the Court concluded that in those cases where the legislators allow exempting part of the land from taxation, they expressly state so. However, the Court did not observe that the two exemptions in question have entirely different purposes. While the exemption of agricultural land on which the agricultural production ceased is of a corrective nature – i.e. the situation where land does not generate any income from agricultural activity – the second exemption was introduced to encourage taxpayers to set up new holdings and expand the existing ones. In a later resolution, the Supreme Administrative Court stated that the legislative organs did not want to adopt a decision that would exempt a part of the land which did not exceed

26 The resolution of the Supreme Administrative Court of October 19, 1997, ref. no. FPK 14/97, CBOSA.

27 See more in: K. Deputat, J. Orłowski, "Zwolnienie od podatku rolnego w przypadku utworzenia nowego lub powiększenia już istniejącego gospodarstwa rolnego," *Finanse Komunalne*, No. 2 (2000), pp. 29–31.

28 See: Art. 12 section 1, point 7 of the Agricultural Tax Act.

the area of 100 ha of the farm, with simultaneous taxation of the land surplus.[29] However, there is no direct reference to such a problem in the parliamentary transcripts on which the Court based.[30] The Supreme Administrative Court noted that the phrase "up to an area not exceeding 100 ha" was in that part of the provision, which refers to the premise for the exemption, i.e. to the area of the holding, and not to the territory acquired or obtained in permanent usufruct. We should state that the above interpretations discriminate against taxpayers who purchase land that will slightly exceed the 100-ha limit. In such a case, purchasing a 100 ha of land to enlarge an agricultural holding of 1,01 ha will make benefiting from the exemption impossible. Using language interpretation and parliamentary transcripts, which do not directly refer to the problem, distorts the aim of improving the agrarian structure of Polish agriculture. It should be emphasized that tax privileges – as the exemption in question – are a kind of indirect subsidy from public authorities. Therefore, the purpose of the tax preference should be momentous. Given the fact that the agrarian structure is weak, a flawed interpretation of tax regulations destroys both the importance and the meaning of the exemption itself. We also should assess the discussed interpretations critically in the context of systemic solutions of Polish tax law. The solutions are contrary to similar regulations contained in other tax laws. In general, in Polish tax law, the phrase "exemption (...) up to an amount not exceeding (...)" means that the tax privilege indicated by the Act may be used up to the amount specified by the legal norm, while the so-called surplus is subject to general taxation rules. Therefore, the subject literature rightly calls the validity of the interpretation of courts and tax authorities into question.[31] It seems that in the face of the above arguments, the taxpayer's interest should guide the authorities making interpretations.

In case of applying the exemption to land intended for establishing a new agricultural holding or extending an existing one to an area not exceeding 100 ha, the form of obtaining the right to the land is a crucial premise. The provisions of the Agricultural Tax Act state that land intended for establishing a new agricultural holding or extending an existing one which is subject to property rights,

---

29 The judgment of the Supreme Administrative Court of May 4, 1999, ref. no. FPS 21/98, CBOSA; the judgment of the Voivodeship Administrative Court in Szczecin of April 29, 2015, ref. no. I SA/Sz 186/15, CBOSA.

30 Transcript 79 from the parliament's session of May 8, 1996, No. 119 (242) II term of the Sejm.

31 L. Etel, *Podatki od nieruchomości* (Warsaw, 2009), p. 373.

or rights of perpetual usufruct, acquired through a sales contract, is exempt. Consequently, land which was acquired as a result of *inter vivos* or *mortis causa* operations cannot benefit from the exemption in question. The Act clearly indicates that the only way of acquisition is through a sales contract. However, in practice, the phrase "acquired through a sales contract" raised many questions of interpretation. It was often broadly understood as any kind of sale, including the acquisition of land by auction. However, it seems that the provisions of the Agricultural Tax Act are exact, indicating that land can only be acquired through a sales contract. The regulations must also be interpreted in this way.

A person may not apply the exemption if the land to create a new agricultural holding or to extend an existing one was acquired under a sales contract from, among others, the taxpayer's spouse. Therefore, there is a doubt as to how to interpret the above legal regulations. It is a rule that joint marital ownership arises when spouses enter the marriage.[32] However, the Family and Guardianship Code also provides for the possibility to exclude the joint marital ownership by concluding a relevant agreement. Concluding such an agreement results in creating two separate estates and autonomizing them regardless of the relations between the spouses. Therefore, each of the spouses may freely dispose of their property, selling it, encumbering it with rights or freely appoint testators. Such a situation raises the question whether a tax exemption may or may not be granted if spouses conclude a contract for property separation and one spouse sells the land to the other. The Agricultural Tax Act does not regulate the mentioned issues. The Act only states that the purchase of land by way of a sales contract between spouses does not entitle to benefit from the exemption in question. However, in the Act, there is no provision for the possibility that the conclusion of marriage itself may give rise to two distinct situations in terms of property relationships. One case is that in exemption based on the joint marital ownership agreement in the law and property scope, spouses remain strangers to each other. It seems that in such a case, it is just to separately treat a spouse who has a part in the joint marital property, and a spouse with whom an agreement on the exemption of such a community was made. However, such interpretation bases on the fact that – apart from the spouse – the sellers of agricultural land cannot be persons who are more or less related to the taxpayer. Such persons are the spouse of a relative in a straight line, stepson, son-in-law, and daughter-in-law.

32 Art. 31 of the Act of February 25, 1964 on Family and Guardianship Code (Journal of Laws 2017, item 682).

The third essential premise is the purpose of acquiring or obtaining the land for permanent development. The purpose of acquiring or obtaining the land must be to establish a new or extend an existing agricultural holding to benefit from the exemption. Thus, an exemption in agricultural tax appertains in such cases which lead to permanent solutions improving the agrarian structure of the country. Let us now clarify the notion of "obtaining land for permanent development." We should understand the notion as obtaining land for lease or use for a period not shorter than ten years. Given the above, the termination of a ten-year lease contract nullifies the premise for granting the exemption. Thus, a situation arises where the temporary condition necessary for land development to become permanent is not met.

Apart from an extensive list of tax exemptions, the Agricultural Tax Act also provides for a set of **tax reliefs**, which are:

1) relief for the occurrence of a natural disaster;
2) relief in relation to land located in submontane and mountainous regions;
3) investment relief.

Ad. 1. The tax authority may grant the taxpayer relief in case of introducing an emergency state due to a natural disaster. The Act of April 18, 2002 defines an emergency state introduced due to a natural disaster. The emergency state due to a natural disaster may be introduced to prevent the effects of natural disasters or technical failures happening due to a natural disaster and to remove them. On the other hand, we should understand the notion as a natural disaster or technical failure, the effects of which: threaten the life or health of a large number of people, property of large sizes or the environment in large areas; only the use of extraordinary measures can aid and protection, in cooperation with various bodies and institutions, and specialized services and formations operating under uniform management. Granting the relief to a taxpayer consists in ceasing the tax assessment or in stopping tax collection in whole or in part when the decision imposing the agricultural tax was already notified to the taxpayer. The amount of relief depends on the extent of losses caused by a natural disaster in an agricultural holding. When granting the relief, the tax authority must consider the amount of compensation received under the statutory insurance. The relief is granted at the taxpayer's request for the tax year in which the natural disaster occurred. If the disaster occurs after paying the tax for a given year, then relief applies to the following year.

Ad. 2. A relief in relation to land located in submontane and mountainous regions consists in reducing the tax by 30 % for the land of class I, II, IIIa, and III by 60 % for the land of class IVa, IV, and IVb located in submontane and mountainous regions. According to the Agricultural Tax Act, submontane and mountainous regions are such localities where at least 50 % of the agricultural land is located above 350 m above sea level.[33] Introducing the above relief into the agricultural tax results from the fact that the location of the area and its slope has an impact on the revenue from a given usable agricultural land. To obtain an appropriate level of revenue from the land located in submontane or mountainous areas, entities conducting agricultural activity must engage more work and capital.

Ad. 3. The investment relief applies to taxpayers on account of the expenditure incurred on the construction and modernization of livestock buildings used for the husbandry, breeding, and keeping of livestock, as well as environmental protection facilities. Moreover, the investment relief will also apply to those taxpayers who decide to purchase and install sprinklers, drainage devices, and water supply devices for agricultural holdings and devices for producing natural energy out of sources like wind, biogas, sun, or water drop.

The Agricultural Tax Act does not define the basic terms related to the scope of the relief in question. Therefore, relief application often raises many interpretation doubts. While the term "construction" does not provoke major problems, they may happen in the case of the "modernization" of livestock buildings term. Due to the lack of regulation of the term "modernization" in the Agricultural Tax Act, we should find its meaning in a dictionary. The word "modernization" means the Act of modernizing, making something contemporary.[34] Therefore, we should understand the term "modernization of livestock buildings" as works aimed at improving the construction or installing modern equipment. Since the Agricultural Tax Act does not define the concept of a livestock building, we should clarify that in such a case, we should understand the term "livestock building" as buildings used for breeding, husbandry, and keeping livestock. Although the word "inventory" applies to the livestock and the so-called deadstock (e.g. combine harvesters, tractors), a relief applies to livestock buildings, i.e., among other things, poultry houses, barns, pigsties, stables, fattening houses.

Modernization works should aim to increase the use-value of the building and thus contribute directly or indirectly to improving the quality of agricultural production or reducing costs associated with it. According to the thesis contained in the judgment of one of the Voivodeship Administrative Courts, works that have an impact on improving the functionality, appearance, durability, and usefulness

---

33 Art. 13b of the Agricultural Tax Act.

34 P. Skorupka, H. Anderska, Z. Łempicka (eds.), *Mały słownik…*, p. 399.

of the building also are of modernizing character.[35] Noteworthy, the modernization of livestock buildings should concern the substance of the building and not its equipment, which is separate movables.[36] Thus, the purchase of various types of equipment for improving agricultural production not permanently connected with the building does not entitle to benefit from the relief in question. The relevant literature emphasizes that the relief is possible after the modernization of mixed-type buildings, i.e. inventory and storage buildings, concerning the part of the modernized building, which has an inventory character.[37] The provisions of the Agricultural Tax Act also do not specify the notion of "environmental protection facilities." According to the dictionary, "protection" is the Act of keeping safe from destruction, damage, danger; what protects, what keeps safe.[38] It seems that such objects are buildings and structures whose purpose is to protect the natural environment against possible degradation resulting from the side effect of agricultural production. Therefore, to benefit from the relief, the environmental facility must protect the environment from degradation. Thus, sewage treatment plants, manure slabs, slurry tanks, gas boiler plants can be environmental protection facilities. Such objects minimize the negative impact of agricultural production on the natural environment. However, such objects do not always significantly improve the condition of the natural environment.

The phrase "purchase and installation of drainage and water supply equipment" raises many problems. Problems arise because the Agricultural Tax Act does not specify the meaning of "drainage facilities." The Agricultural Tax Act also does not define the term "water supply equipment for farms." Nevertheless, the interpretation should not cause major problems.[39] Such devices are public wells, devices for water abstraction and intake, water supply networks.

---

35 The judgment of the Voivodeship Administrative Court in Olsztyn of April 4, 2005, ref. no. I SA/Ol 359/04, CBOSA.

36 The judgment of the Supreme Administrative Court of October 14, 1998, ref. no. III SA 1565/97, CBOSA.

37 B. Pahl, "Ulga inwestycyjna w podatku rolnym-problemy praktyczne," *Finanse Komunalne*, No. 10 (2007), pp. 29–30.

38 P. Skorupka, H. Anderska, Z. Łempicka (eds.), *Mały słownik…*, p. 477.

39 See more in: K. Mrozik, "Zakup i zainstalowanie urządzeń melioracyjnych i urządzeń zaopatrzenia gospodarstwa w wodę a ulga inwestycyjna w podatku rolnym," *Przegląd Podatków Lokalnych i Finansów Samorządowych*, No. 7–8 (2008), p. 20. See also: the judgment of the Supreme Administrative Court of February 23, 1994, ref. no. III SA 1297/93, CBOSA. In the judgment, the Supreme Administrative Court stated that the investment tax relief in the agricultural tax also applies to those taxpayers who incurred expenses for installing the agricultural holding's water supply facilities within

However, granting investment relief due to the purchase and assembly of equipment to be used for producing energy out of renewable sources, and sprinkler systems is not in doubt. A sprinkling system is a mechanical device that sprays water in the form of artificial rain and consists of a pumping station, water supply network, and sprinklers. The device helps in surface irrigation of field crops, orchards, vineyards, and meadows.[40]

The investment relief applies after completion of the investment. The relief consists in deducting 25 % of the investment outlays documented with investment bills from the due agricultural tax on the land located in the commune where the investment took place.

The amount of investment relief is deducted ex officio. Taxpayers who, under the Agricultural Tax Act, must submit agricultural tax returns, deduct the amount of the relief granted from the tax due.[41] Selling facilities and equipment on which the investment relief was granted will result in the taxpayer losing the unused amount of the relief.[42] In the case of unused investment relief, it may transfer to the legal successors of the taxpayer if the agricultural holding was acquired by inheritance or on the basis of social security regulations of farmers.[43] Noteworthy, the investment relief is not available to taxpayers whose expenditure for the investment implementation financed in whole or in part from public funds. It seems that nowadays, the investment relief does not meet its expectations and favors large area holdings. Even with high investment outlays related to construction or modernization of livestock buildings, taxpayers are not always able to fully deduct the outlays incurred under the relief granted. What is more, it is difficult to talk about covering costs related to investments on the farm. The scope of the relief is also in doubt. In practice, the agricultural tax charges mainly plant production. However, the taxpayer cannot take advantage of the relief consisting in building facilities for plant production. Moreover, the regulations contained in the Agricultural Tax Act do not notice the problem of investments related to ecological farming, so actively promoted in the European Union in recent years.

---

acting in the social committee for the construction of a water supply system, even if the commune's budget financed such construction.

40 K. Gawrońska, "Ulga inwestycyjna w podatku rolnym," *Przegląd Podatków Lokalnych i Finansów Samorządowych*, No. 3 (2009), p. 13.

41 Art. 13 section 3a of the Agricultural Tax Act.

42 Art. 13 section 4 of the Agricultural Tax Act.

43 Art. 13d section 5 of the Agricultural Tax Act.

V. Tax base

The tax base amount depends on whether the object of taxation is part of an agricultural holding. For the land not forming part of an agricultural holding, the tax base is the area of land **expressed in physical hectares**. The base results from the Land and Property Register.

Concerning the land forming part of the agricultural holding, the tax base represents the area of land **expressed in conversion hectares**. Conversion hectare is a special unit set exclusively for agricultural tax purposes. The purpose of introducing the conversion hectare into the agricultural tax's construction was to take account of the differences in agricultural revenue of individual holdings. As is well known, such differences in agricultural production result not only from the size of the holding but also from its geographical location, climatic conditions, the hydrological conditions of the area, the types of agricultural land, or the land's quality. Moreover, different economic conditions play an important role in diversifying the revenue of agricultural holdings. Therefore, it was decided to build the tax base on a special unit to spread the tax burden properly. The conversion hectare bases on such factors as the **type and class of the usable agricultural land**, or the proper inclusion **in the tax district**.[44]

Four tax districts were established in the country to diversify the revenue of agricultural holdings. The districts include towns and communes. The appropriate assignment of an administrative unit to one of the tax districts bases on economic and production-climatic factors. Each factor is important. The economic factor plays a crucial role in relation to the level of production and income from it. The agrarian structure, agricultural strength resources, economic level of the region, degree of industrialization, level of infrastructure, availability of sales market, and technical equipment have a significant impact on assigning a particular administrative unit to a given tax district based on the factor mentioned above. Not relying on the above considerations when including an administrative unit in one of the four tax districts would result in disparities in the tax burden. Agricultural holdings located in communes or towns with a higher degree of industrialization or infrastructure and large and absorbent market have an economic advantage over those with a lesser location. Such a situation results, for example, from the fact that the costs of agricultural production in areas with a higher economic level are lower. Thus, lower costs of production enable higher revenue of agricultural holdings.

---

44 Ordinance of the Minister of Finance of December 10, 2001 on the classification of communes and towns into one of four tax districts (Journal of Laws 2001, No. 143, item 1614).

The production and climate factor also strongly influences qualifying a given commune or town to a proper district. Not considering the factor would result in increasing the tax burden on weaker farms in comparison to stronger ones. The reason for such a situation is that natural conditions in individual regions of the country vary. Essential criteria, considering the production and climatic factor in this case, are, among other things, agricultural suitability of soils, terrain shape, or hydrological conditions. Noteworthy, in Polish climatic and soil conditions, using the maximum of agrotechnical solutions, we can obtain high crops with adequately abundant water resources in the soil. Thermal and radiation conditions play a significant role in plant production only when the soil is sufficiently moistened. The moisture depends on precipitation, which is the primary source of water supply for the soil. Moreover, the quality of the soil itself depends on whether the soil is well moistened. Climatic conditions during the vegetative period of the plants also play a vital role in obtaining sufficiently high crops.

Assigning individual communes and towns to appropriate tax districts that depend on economic and production-climatic conditions is extremely important in differentiating the revenue of agricultural holdings across the country.[45] An additional differentiating element is the division of agricultural land into types. Usable agricultural land divides into arable land, and meadows and pastures. Every kind of usable agricultural land qualifies to separate tax districts. Therefore, there are four tax districts established for agricultural land and four for meadows and pastures. From a theoretical point of view, arable land is used to grow more profitable crops such as wheat, rye, and potatoes. Meanwhile, meadows and pastures are used for grazing or for growing crops that are a source of animal nutrition. It is also often the case that wheat, rye, or potatoes grow on usable agricultural land classified in the Land and Property Register as meadows and pastures.

The last criterion for converting a physical hectare into a conversion hectare is the division of the usable agricultural area into valuation classes, which reflect its agricultural value. The division happens on the basis of classes' characteristics and the natural conditions of the usable land. When determining the characteristics of soils, the factors which determine the assignment to the appropriate class are, among other things, land's mineral composition and water permeability.

45 M. Podstawka, "Podatek rolny od gruntów – jego ocena i potrzeba zmian," *Roczniki Naukowe SERiA* Vol. 7, part 4, (2005), pp. 347–351.

We can observe that the diversification of agricultural holdings' revenue in terms of agricultural tax considering the production and climatic factor takes place twice. First, the very division into valuation classes causes proper classification of land in terms of its agricultural usefulness. The division, as we know, apart from the mineral values of soils or their permeability, also considers such a factor as land location. Second, the differentiation of land in agricultural holdings on the basis of the valuation classes further verifies within the tax districts, where climatic and soil conditions, land location, and water relations are also considered.

The very fact of reckoning differences in revenue between agricultural holdings in Poland, and thus their tax burden is done at two levels. The first level is a common, nationwide variation of hectare conversion rates by tax districts. Additionally, the agricultural tax introduces a relief concerning land located in mountainous and submontane areas.[46]

The second method of determining the differences in revenue applies locally by the voivodeship government assembly at the request of the commune council. The method consists in moving the commune to another tax district. Such a transfer may take place only in economically justified cases after consultation with the chamber of agriculture. However, the Agricultural Tax Act introduces certain restrictions in this respect. Restrictions consist in the fact that the transfer of a commune from one tax district to another cannot reduce the number of conversion hectares for the voivodeship, in which the commune is, by more than 1.5 %.[47] The same situation may happen if another tax district includes some villages within a commune. There also is a limitation to the reduction of conversion hectares number to 1.5 % in such a situation. The commune council transfers individual villages to another tax district after consulting with the chamber of agriculture.[48]

Determining the taxable amount in the agricultural tax consists in multiplying the physical hectares of an agricultural holding by the conversion rate assigned for agricultural use. The highest rates refer to the best usable agricultural land located in the first tax district. Thus, the amount of tax imposed on such a usable area will be higher than on the lowest classified agricultural land, meadows, and pastures.

46 Art. 13b of the Agricultural Tax Act.

47 Art. 5 section 2 of the Agricultural Tax Act.

48 See: L. Etel, *Uchwały podatkowe samorządu terytorialnego* (Białystok, 2004), pp. 166–167.

In the case of **horticultural production**, the tax base results from multiplying physical hectares by the conversion rates used for arable land.[49] Applying the above solutions in relation to horticultural production seems to be controversial since such a type of production is, as a rule, more economically efficient than other crop production and can be run on a smaller area. Moreover, orchard holdings with an average area of usable agricultural land of about 21 ha and above obtain full profitability. Such orchards are profitable and able to invest in modern production solutions.[50] Noteworthy, the previous regulations in the field of agricultural taxation recognized the horticultural activity as specialized agricultural production[51] and assumed that the income obtained from the activity was higher than the average income earned from other agricultural production. Given the increased payment capacity achieved by holdings engaged in horticultural production, it was necessary to qualify such activities as special branches of agricultural production.[52]

We should positively refer to the regulations under which conversion rates were set for built-up, wooded, and bushed land on usable agricultural land and land under ditches. As a general rule, the area mentioned above does not generate revenue, the amount of which depends on the quality of the land, so it is not justified to apply conversion rates relating to the conversion hectare to such types of land. Therefore, it is rightly assumed that 1 hectare of built-up agricultural land constitutes 1 conversion hectare. On the other hand, 1 hectare of wooded and planted land constitutes 0.20 conversion hectare. We should consider such a solution appropriate because most often such land is not used for agricultural production purposes, and thus does not constitute, or very rarely constitutes a source of revenue.

Separate rules are applied when setting conversion rates for land under ponds. Solutions introduced January 1, 2016, tell that 1 ha of land under the non-stockinged pond constitutes 0.2 conversion ha. In the case of the pond stocked with salmon, sea trout, huchen, lake trout, and trout, 1 ha equals 1 conversion ha,

49 Art. 5 section 6 of the Agricultural Tax Act. When applying conversion rates to class III and IV orchards, the conversion rates for class IIIa and IVa should be applied respectively.

50 J. Sobierajewska, "Analiza efektywności polskich gospodarstw sadowniczych na przykładzie gospodarstw z regionu Mazowsze i Podlasie," *Roczniki Naukowe Stowarzyszenia Ekonomistów Rolnictwa i Agrobiznesu*, Vol. 11, part 1, (2009), pp. 389–393.

51 See: Ordinance of the Council of Ministers of December 8, 1971 on the taxation of special branches with land tax (Journal of Laws No. 34, item 300 as amended).

52 M. Pietrewicz, "Opodatkowanie działów specjalnych w indywidualnych gospodarstwach rolnych," *Finanse*, No. 12 (1975), pp. 35 ff.

while 1 ha of the pond stocked with other fish species is equivalent to 0.20 conversion ha. In a given case, it is irrelevant which tax district the commune, town, or village is in.[53] Moreover, we only can refer to the land under a pond within the meaning provided by the Agricultural Tax Act if it was marked in the Land and Property Register.[54] As a result, land under any other water bodies intended for fish farming, which are not marked in the Land and Property Register with the Wsr symbol, should be subject to property tax.[55]

Noteworthy, the conversion hectare is a special unit created to measure the tax base. Conversion hectare considers, in an estimated manner, differences in the profitability of individual agricultural holdings characterized by crop production. It is an unfortunate solution to use a conversion hectare with such a low conversion rate to determine the estimated revenue from breeding all fish species. Applying the conversion hectare criterion created for crop production, and carp and trout farming does not take proper account of the payment capacity of individual farm types.

The method of determining the tax base using the so-called "externalities" should apply as a last resort. However, despite drawbacks, the Polish agricultural tax considers such factors that have a significant impact on plant production. Dividing agricultural land into classes, types, and tax districts depending on economic and production-climatic conditions causes that the agricultural tax differentiates agricultural holdings in terms of production possibilities. The main disadvantage of such a tax is the lack of direct animal production taxation.

VI. The structure of the tax scale

In the agricultural tax, the tax rate depends on the current price for a quintal of rye calculated according to the average purchase price for the 11 quarters preceding the quarter preceding the tax year. The average purchase price determines

53 Art. 5 section 7 of the Agricultural Tax Act.

54 See: L. Etel, "Definicja gospodarstwa rolnego w podatku rolnym – problemy praktyczne," in: *Podatki i opłaty lokalne w praktyce*, ed. M. Popławski (Warsaw, 2008), pp. 42–44.

55 R. Dowgier, M. Popławski, "Opodatkowanie gruntów pod wodami – wybrane problemy," *Finanse Komunalne*, No. 9 (2006), p. 22. To cover the agricultural tax on land under water not classified as land under the ponds, it is necessary to reclassify the land or to carry out a counter-evidence, for example, in the form of an expert opinion. See also: I. Czaja-Hliniak, "Zasady opodatkowania wód stojących podatku gruntowym," *Gospodarka Rybna*, No. 6 (1984), pp. 13–15; M. Błażejczak, "Rybacki podatek gruntowy w projekcie nowego systemu opodatkowania rolnictwa," *Gospodarka Rybna*, No. 9 (1983), pp. 7–8.

on the basis of the announcement of the President of Statistics Poland. Under the provisions of the Agricultural Tax Act, the commune council can reduce the rye purchase price.[56] In such a context, we should consider whether it is right to grant the commune council the competence to reduce the rye purchase price. Adopting a resolution in this respect significantly influences the amount of the agricultural tax burden. Assuming that the tax in question is a tribute that is imposed on revenue obtained from conducting an agricultural activity, the reduction in the purchase price of rye may affect the competitiveness of individual farms. Such a situation concerns mainly large area farms for which the reduction of the agricultural tax amount may constitute real savings. Under the currently binding regulations, there is a situation where on the territory of the state there is a differentiation in the tax burden on revenues of agricultural holdings running the production of the same crops. It seems that the discussed solutions should not take place in taxes, which, basing on externalities, burden the revenue from agricultural production. The only criteria differentiating the revenue of an agricultural holding should be the types of usable agricultural land, the valuation class, and belonging to tax districts. The possibility of reducing the tax rate could take place in a situation where the agricultural tax is a typical property tax without revenue-income elements. In such a case, the revenue from agricultural activity would have to be subject to income tax.

The type of rate depends on whether the usable agricultural land constitutes an agricultural holding within the meaning of the Agricultural Tax Act. In the case of **land forming a holding**, the tax rate is equivalent of **2.5 quintals of rye** per 1 conversion hectare in cash. For land classified as usable agricultural land, and wooded and bushed area, which **does not constitute an agricultural holding**, the tax rate per 1 hectare is equivalent to **5 quintals** of rye in cash.[57] Introducing the above solution was intended to prevent the tax burden from being reduced over time and to keep the tax burden stable. Relying the tax assessment on the price of rye justifies in such a way that in the 1980s, this crop was one of the most commonly cultivated in agricultural holdings. Today, according to data provided by the Statistics Poland, rye only ranks ninth in terms of the crop production volume in Poland.[58]

---

56 See: L. Etel, *Uchwały podatkowe samorządu terytorialnego* (Białystok, 2004), pp. 132–133; P. Stanisławiszyn, "Wykonywanie władztwa podatkowego przez gminy po nowelizacji przepisów w 2002 roku w świetle orzecznictwa regionalnych izb obrachunkowych," *Finanse Komunalne*, No. 6 (2003), pp. 13–27.

57 Art. 6 section 1 and 2 of the Agricultural Tax Act.

58 *Statistical Yearbook of Agriculture*, Statistics Poland (Warsaw, 2015), p. 168.

Besides, we should point out that the smaller holdings with lower productivity fell stronger the burden established the way mentioned above. Such a situation results from implementing the stimulative function of the agricultural tax. Stimulative function's assumption was to promote economically stronger and larger holdings. The process of stimulation was to take place by eliminating weaker farms with a relatively higher tax burden.[59] After several decades of the agricultural tax rate based on the price of rye, we must conclude that the objective pursued by the then legislature did not fulfill. The current principle of taxation based on the price of only one agricultural product, i.e. rye, means that agricultural holdings' production is not appropriately taxed.[60] While such a construction is justified in the case of agricultural holdings specializing in the rye production, holdings with other crops are unreliably taxed. We will see such a conclusion in particular if we consider the fact that today's production of rye as part of all field crops in Poland, as previously mentioned, plays a smaller role.

The disadvantage of the tax scale structure is also that, in the case of horticultural crops, relying on the price of rye has no connection whatsoever with the actual revenue generated from such a production. A similar situation happens in the case of other crops. Therefore, it seems appropriate that the tax rate should base on the average price of more agricultural products such as rye, wheat, potatoes, oats, or sugar beet. At the same time, however, horticultural production should base on the average price of fruit, such as apples, cherries, pears, and plums. For fish farms, the rate of agricultural tax could be established basing on the average price of fish farmed in ponds.

VII. Final remarks

The analysis of the current Agricultural Tax Act provisions leads first of all to one basic thesis – the Act is an archaic construction that does not correspond to the current conditions of the free market economy. Nevertheless, we can indicate a few critical and detailed comments.

First, the Act defines the object of taxation incorrectly. The agricultural tax should concern only the land used for purposes of agricultural activity. Therefore, the definition of an agricultural holding as well as an agricultural activity should change. However, the definition should be identical to the income tax definition.

---

59 M. Pietrewicz, *Obciążenia podatkowe rolnictwa indywidualnego i uspołecznionego* (Warsaw, 1988), pp. 82–83.

60 J. Bieluk, "Cena żyta jako miernik wysokości podatku rolnego," *Studia Iuridica Agraria*, No. 1 (2000), pp. 173–178.

Second, agricultural tax preferentially applies to land that is not used for agricultural purposes in any way.

Third, we need to be critical of the adopted tax base form. The tax base depends on the area expressed in conversion hectares, which, in principle, should account for the estimated revenue of the farm. However, we should indicate that, as a result of the outdated concept that the revenue of an agricultural holding determines through external features, i.e. land, not every type of production was taxed. Such a situation applies in particular to animal production.

Fourth, the shape and validity of some of the tax exemptions contained in the construction of the agricultural tax are questionable. Objections may happen because of, among other things, exempting the land of class V, VI, and VIz from taxation, the lack of narrowing the exemptions relating to agricultural production only to entities conducting an agricultural activity, or the existence of provisions which, in their current form, deform the purpose for which some of the exemptions were introduced.

Fifth, objections may happen because of tax reliefs' construction. Noteworthy, the so-called investment relief should also apply to livestock buildings used for plant production. Moreover, the provisions relating to the relief for the occurrence of a natural disaster also need adjustment. Due to the changes made by the legislator, such preference should be eliminated, or the legislation should amend it in such a way that taxpayers can actually benefit from it.

Sixth, we should criticize the concept of setting the tax rate on the basis of the price of one agricultural product only. It seems that the rate should base on the price of essential agricultural products. In the case of horticultural or fish production, a rate based on the average price of fruit or fish farmed in ponds may be appropriate.

The detailed conclusions set out above allow for a general deduction of "the law as it should stand" nature. It seems that the agricultural tax should not be of a revenue-income character, but only a property tax. However, for this to happen, revenue obtained from conducting agricultural activity should be subject to PIT and CIT. On the other hand, the agricultural tax itself should undergo a gradual process of limiting its subjective and objective scope and, consequently, liquidation. Moreover, the whole process should be evolutionary; i.e. it should spread over several years. We will present the main directions for such a process in the conclusions of this monograph.

Conclusion

The past Polish experience confirms the thesis that taxation of agriculture is a very controversial issue of tax law. It is not an easy task to create a rational tax system that would consider both the economic interest of the state and the specificity of agricultural production. In the taxation sphere, typically, legal, economic, social, and political issues intertwine very intensively. Such a situation makes the discussion on the matter in question in Poland lasts so long and is extremely difficult. Many different concepts emerge, often mutually exclusive. The high political risk of such a reform is also of great importance in this respect. For such reasons, an attitude of concern still prevails when concerning the implementation of thorough agricultural taxation reform. Moreover, a strong tendency to favor farmers and agricultural activities makes it difficult to make the reform as well. The trend expresses in the fact that the system of public levies is maintained, in which, as a matter of principle, farmers are subject to a much lower tax burden. Undoubtedly, in Polish conditions, the agricultural tax is not only an archaic structure, – adopted in the period of the centrally planned economy, i.e. Poland in the eighties of the last century – but also a tribute of exceptionally low fiscal efficiency. Nevertheless, there is still a relatively wide range of detailed solutions – e.g. reliefs and exemptions in particular taxes – dedicated to farmers, which put this group of taxpayers in a much better tax and legal position than other taxpayers conducting other forms of economic activity.

There is a **specific duality** of regulations in the area of agricultural activity taxation in Poland. In fact, traditional agricultural activity excludes from income tax. In principle, the agricultural tax is a tribute which is supposed to include both revenue obtained from agricultural production, and the land used for this purpose. Revenue earned from the specialized agricultural activity is subject to PIT or CIT. In such a context, a fundamental question arises about the role and legal nature of the agricultural tax, especially concerning the regulation of both income taxes. The inconsistency of Polish tax regulations against the general principles of agricultural activity taxation applied in other European Union countries is also noticeable. The fiscal effectiveness and the coherence of the adopted and implemented assumptions, both in terms of agricultural and tax policy of Polish regulations, raises doubts.

The specific conditions of conducting agricultural activity favor the formulation of numerous theories concerning the method, scope, and function of taxation of this sphere of taxpayers' activity. A relatively wide range of possible criteria for shaping the amount of tax obligation remains for use. This enables creating various concepts of public levies burdening agricultural activity. It seems that, first of all, depending on the importance of agricultural production in the economy of a given country, prevailing climatic conditions, terrain, as well as the degree of technological advancement, it is possible to separate different models of agricultural taxation. It is characteristic that usually, each tax model consists of two tributes. As a rule, it is a parallel system of charging income and property tax on real estate used in agricultural production. Of course, such a solution does not mean that entities conducting agricultural activity cannot pay other taxes, e.g. indirect taxes or taxes on movable property – it still is in line with the principle of taxation universality. However, basing a given model of taxation on the two levies mentioned above results from the fact that they are, in a way, directly addressed to agriculture – and additionally, they consider the specificity of such a form of activity to a high degree. The other levies which relate directly or indirectly to agricultural operations are, in principle, complementary to the two taxes indicated above. We adopted such an assumption also to set out the main directions of changes in the taxation of agricultural activity in Poland. It seems that in the Polish conditions, it is necessary to move towards solutions under which income obtained from conducting agricultural activity will be subject to income tax. Concerning entities running agricultural activity, in such a model, some variable elements of the income tax structure should be shaped in a slightly different way than for entities conducting non-agricultural economic activity. Entities that achieve high revenue in the tax year should be treated on the same principles as taxpayers conducting non-agricultural economic activity. Regardless of that, agricultural land should be subject to real estate tax (with the tax base determined by the value of the real estate).

Concerning social conditions, as well as mostly political ones, the introduction of the target model of agricultural taxation in Poland should be spread over time. An appropriate period of *vacatio legis* is necessary, and the whole process should take place in several stages. It seems that a rational division into three stages is possible. The total time of the reform should close within fifteen years.

In the first stage of the reform (lasting about five years), the extent of the tax burden should be clearly differentiated depending on whether agricultural land will be used for agricultural activities. Achieving the above objective will be possible by introducing the concept of an agricultural entrepreneur into the construction of the agricultural tax and changing the definition of an agricultural holding, which should be understood as land classified in the land and building register as agricultural land related to running an agricultural activity.

An essential element of the agricultural activity definition that should be introduced in the first stage of the reform is the concept of an agricultural entrepreneur. It should be stressed that only entities that acquire the above status will be able to run agricultural activity on the basis of agricultural tax, but also income taxes. According to the adopted concept of an agricultural entrepreneur, it will be possible to become one for: a natural person, a legal person, an organizational unit without legal personality, which, regardless of the result, conducts agricultural activity and which will enter the register of agricultural entrepreneurs. The obligation to obtain the status of an agricultural entrepreneur should be imposed on entities that already led agricultural activity – including special branches of agricultural production – in the year preceding the introduction of the first stage of the reform, and express their will to continue it in the following years. Moreover, entities, who will start conducting agricultural activity after the implementation of the reform's first stage will be obliged to obtain the status of an agricultural entrepreneur. Agricultural activity, in this regard, will be defined as:

1) activity consisting in producing plant and animal products in an unprocessed state from own crops, breeding or husbandry;
2) processing of plant and animal products within the conducted agricultural holding in a manner other than industrial, specified in the regulation issued by the agriculture minister, coming from own crops, breeding or husbandry, provided that their quantity constitutes at least 50 % of a given product, excluding water.

Detailed procedures related to the conditions under which interested parties could acquire the status of agricultural entrepreneur should be developed once a decision is taken on the reform aimed at implementing the target model. At this point, we can only point certain minimum requirements that an entity applying for the status of an agricultural entrepreneur should meet. First, an entry in the register of agricultural entrepreneurs should be made at the request of the entity itself. Second, keeping the register should be the responsibility of the head of a commune, mayor, or city president. Third, the application for entry should include in particular: the name of the entity applying for admission; address of the place of residence or seat; identification number of the taxpayer; an indication of the head of the tax office competent for the place of residence or seat; national court register number in case of legal persons; an indication of the type of the performed plant or animal production; and in case of conducting the agricultural activity, within the framework of which usable agricultural land is used – information about the area of agricultural land, as of the date of application submission, being in possession of perpetual usufruct, self-owned or dependent type.

Due to introducing the changes mentioned above in the first stage, the agricultural tax, depending on the type of taxpayer, will have a twofold character for several years. In relation to taxpayers having the status of agricultural entrepreneurs, it would still be a tax of revenue and income nature. Taxpayers who are agricultural entrepreneurs would still be able to use the benefits of the existing tax exemptions, investment relief, and mountain and submontane relief. The tax base should be expressed in conversion hectares, and the tax rate should be determined basing on a set of crops commonly cultivated in Poland. However, concerning taxpayers who will not have the status of an agricultural entrepreneur, the agricultural tax should have the character of a property tax with the tax base expressed in physical hectares. Such taxpayers could only benefit from exemptions relating to the land which they could not freely dispose of for reasons beyond their control – e.g. located in a border road strip, constituting ecological land, etc. Also, such taxpayers could not receive tax relief. At the same time, it becomes necessary to eliminate the standards of estimated annual income in special branches of agricultural production, in the construction of the personal income tax.

In the second stage of the reform, the agricultural tax should become a tribute of a property nature, devoid of revenue, and income elements. The aim would be to break with the dichotomy of the agricultural tax introduced at the first stage, i.e. the existence of separate rules for taxation of land forming part of an agricultural holding – possessed by an agricultural entrepreneur – and land not constituting an agricultural holding. This means that the agricultural tax in the new construction should only charge the land classified in the land and building register as usable agricultural land, which is connected with running an agricultural activity, i.e., possessed by an agricultural entrepreneur. On the other hand, land classified in the land and building register as usable agricultural land, which in the first stage of the reform was not part of an agricultural holding, i.e., was not in agricultural entrepreneur's possession, should be excluded from agricultural tax, and be subject to taxation in real estate tax. To ensure that the agricultural tax has a property character, those exemptions of land which in any way relate to its use for agricultural purposes should be eliminated – e.g. exemption of land from the development of wasteland; land obtained by means of exchange or consolidation. The only exemptions which should remain in the construction of the agricultural tax should be those relating to land which the taxpayer cannot dispose of freely for reasons beyond his or her control. The reliefs should be abolished. The taxable amount should base on an area expressed in physical hectares.

The consequence of modifying the legal nature of the agricultural tax, which would constitute a tribute of a property nature, will be **the necessity to tax the revenue from agricultural activity**. Such action should take place both on the grounds of PIT and CIT. Including agricultural activity as the subject of PIT will lead to the fact that it will be unnecessary to tax specialist agricultural activity separately. The tax base for taxpayers conducting agricultural activity should be actual income determined on the basis of tax documentation. A preferential solution addressed to taxpayers conducting agricultural activity should be the possibility to establish lump-sum tax-deductible costs. Only those agricultural entrepreneurs whose revenue in the year preceding the tax year do not exceed PLN 200,000.00 should benefit from the above preference. The amount of lump-sum tax-deductible costs should range from 80 % to 90 % of the obtained revenue. Taxpayers with the status of an agricultural entrepreneur should be entitled to an additional tax preference, consisting in exempting the income which will be spent entirely or in part for investments indicated in the Act. The exemption will be available to an agricultural entrepreneur who will use all or part of his income for investments consisting in: purchasing agricultural land; construction, extension, modernization, or renovation of buildings used for conducting the agricultural activity, both in plant and animal production; purchasing tangible assets such as agricultural machinery. Income obtained from agricultural activity should be exempt from taxation in an amount that corresponds to the product of this income and the share of investment expenditure in the assets used to conduct agricultural activity made by the agricultural producer in income from agricultural activity. Moreover, EU subsidies for agricultural production received by agricultural entrepreneurs should also be exempt from income tax.

The implementation of the **third stage of the reform** means that the target model of taxation of agricultural activities is achieved. We should stress that, while the principles of income taxation adopted in the second stage of the reform will remain unchanged, a significant change will happen in the area of taxation of land used for agricultural activity by eliminating the agricultural tax. Thus, land connected with conducting the agricultural activity, i.e. possessed by an agricultural entrepreneur, will be subject to real estate tax. Implementing the third stage should link with the introduction of a comprehensive real estate taxation reform in Poland. Such an improvement means verifying the current rules of the real estate tax and forestry tax.

Bibliography

Bieluk J., "Cena żyta jako miernik wysokości podatku rolnego", *Studia Iuridica Agraria*, No. 1 (2000).

Błażejczak M., "Rybacki podatek gruntowy w projekcie nowego systemu opodatkowania rolnictwa", *Gospodarka Rybna*, No. 9 (1983).

Borszowski P., K. Stelmaszczyk, *Podatki i opłaty lokalne. Podatek rolny. Podatek leśny. Komentarz* (Warsaw, 2016).

Borszowski P., M. Kowalska, "Podejmowanie działalności gospodarczej a definicja kosztów podatkowych", *Prawo i Podatki*, No. 2 (2009).

Burzec M., "Opodatkowanie dochodu osób fizycznych", in: *Opodatkowanie rolnictwa w Polsce. Weryfikacja założeń. Perspektywa zmian*, ed. P. Smoleń (Warsaw, 2018a), pp. 165–167.

Burzec M., "Podatek rolny", in: *Opodatkowanie rolnictwa w Polsce. Weryfikacja założeń. Perspektywa zmian*, ed. P. Smoleń (Warsaw, 2018b).

Burzec M., "Pojęcie działalności rolniczej na gruncie ustawy o podatku dochodowym od osób fizycznych – wnioski de lege ferenda", *Przegląd Prawa Publicznego*, No. 10 (2017a).

Burzec M., "Taxation of specialist agricultural activity in Poland – an attempt to evaluate the existing solutions", in: *Essential Problems with Taxation of Agriculture*, eds. M. Burzec, P. Smoleń (Lublin, 2017b).

Burzec M., P. Smoleń, *Introduction to Polish Tax Law* (Berlin-New York, 2018a).

Burzec M., P. Smoleń, "Modele opodatkowania rolnictwa", in: *Opodatkowanie rolnictwa w Polsce. Weryfikacja założeń, perspektywa zmian*, ed. P. Smoleń (Warsaw, 2018b).

Czaja-Hliniak I., "Zasady opodatkowania wód stojących podatku gruntowym", *Gospodarka Rybna*, No. 6 (1984).

Deputat K., J. Orłowski, "Zwolnienie od podatku rolnego w przypadku utworzenia nowego lub powiększenia już istniejącego gospodarstwa rolnego", *Finanse Komunalne*, No. 2 (2000).

Dowgier R., M. Popławski, "Opodatkowanie gruntów pod wodami – wybrane problemy", *Finanse Komunalne*, No. 9 (2006).

Duda-Hyz M., "Controversies over the status of flat-rate farmers in Polish Value Added Tax-selected issues", in: *Essential Problems with Taxation of Agriculture*, eds. M. Burzec, P. Smoleń (Lublin, 2017).

Duda-Hyz M., "Szczególna procedura dla rolników ryczałtowych w podatku od towarów i usług", in: *Opodatkowanie rolnictwa w Polsce. Weryfikacja założeń, perspektywa zmian*, ed. P. Smoleń (Warsaw, 2018).

Dzun W., *Gospodarstwa rolne osób prawnych w procesie transformacji systemowej i integracji z UE* (Warsaw, 2015).

Dzun W., *Państwowe gospodarstwa rolne w procesie przemian systemowych w Polsce* (Warsaw, 2005).

Etel L., "Definicja gospodarstwa rolnego w podatku rolnym – problemy praktyczne", in: *Podatki i opłaty lokalne w praktyce*, ed. M. Popławski (Warsaw, 2008).

Etel L., "Podatki przychodowo-dochodowo-majątkowe", in: *System prawa finansowego. Tom III. Prawo daninowe*, eds. L. Etel, J. Głuchowski, C. Kosikowski, E. Ruśkowski (Warsaw, 2010).

Etel L., *Podatek rolny. Podatek leśny. Komentarz* (Warsaw, 2012).

Etel L., *Podatki od nieruchomości* (Warsaw, 2009).

Etel L., *Uchwały podatkowe samorządu terytorialnego* (Białystok, 2004).

Gawrońska K., "Ulga inwestycyjna w podatku rolnym", *Przegląd Podatków Lokalnych i Finansów Samorządowych*, No. 3 (2009).

Gomułowicz A., *Koszty uzyskania przychodów. Zasady ogólne* (Warsaw, 2005).

Gomułowicz A., *Prawna formuła kosztu podatkowego* (Warsaw, 2016).

Górka M., M. Ruda, "Spółdzielcze formy gospodarowania na przykładzie rolniczych spółdzielni produkcyjnych", *Nierówności Społeczne a Wzrost Gospodarczy*, No. 27 (2012).

Guzewicz W., A. Kagan, M. Zdzieborska, *Procesy dostosowawcze w rolniczych spółdzielniach produkcyjnych* (Warsaw, 2005).

Hanusz A., *Polityka podatkowa w zakresie różnicowania obciążeń dochodów rolniczych w Polsce* (Lublin, 1996).

Jóźwiak W., W. Ziętara, *Zmiany zachodzące w gospodarstwach rolnych w latach 2002–2010* (Warsaw, 2013).

Kalinowski M., *Podmiotowość prawna podatnika* (Toruń, 1999).

Kalinowski M., "Rodzaje podatków i ich klasyfikacja oraz systemy podatkowe", in: *System prawa finansowego. Tom III. Prawo daninowe*, eds. L. Etel, J. Głuchowski, C. Kosikowski, E. Ruśkowski (Warsaw, 2010).

Kucia-Guściora B., "Agricultural producer groups in Polish Corporate Income Tax", in: *Essential Problems with Taxation of Agriculture*, eds. M. Burzec, P. Smoleń (Lublin, 2017).

Kucia-Guściora B., "Opodatkowanie dochodu osób prawnych", in: *Opodatkowanie rolnictwa w Polsce. Weryfikacja założeń, perspektywy zmian*, ed. P. Smoleń (Warsaw, 2018).

Kucia-Guściora B., "Węzłowe problemy preferencji podatkowych dla grup producentów rolnych", *Wieś i Rolnictwo*, No. 1 (2019).

Lenio P., "Health Insurance Contributions of Farmers", in: *Essential Problems with Taxation of Agriculture*, eds. M. Burzec, P. Smoleń (Lublin, 2017).

Liszewski G., "Reforma podatku rolnego – próba oceny", in: *Polski system podatkowy. Założenia a praktyka*, ed. A. Pomorska (Lublin, 2004).

Mariański A., W. Nykiel, "Koszty w prawie bilansowym i podatkowym – pojęcie i zasady ich uznawania w zysku i dochodzie", *Kwartalnik Prawa Podatkowego*, No. 1 (2007).

Meinberg P., *Rachunkowość rolnicza* (Warsaw, 1971).

Miemiec W., P. Pest, "The development of agricultural production and refund of excise tax", in: *Essential Problems with Taxation of Agriculture*, eds. M. Burzec, P. Smoleń (Lublin, 2017).

Miemiec W., P. Pest, "Wykorzystywanie oleju napędowego do produkcji rolnej a zwrot podatku akcyzowego", *Kwartalnik Prawno-Finansowy*, No. 1 (2018).

Mrozik K., "Zakup i zainstalowanie urządzeń melioracyjnych i urządzeń zaopatrzenia gospodarstwa w wodę a ulga inwestycyjna w podatku rolnym", *Przegląd Podatków Lokalnych i Finansów Samorządowych*, No. 7–8 (2008).

Münnich M., "Podatek akcyzowy", in: *Opodatkowanie rolnictwa w Polsce. Weryfikacja założeń, perspektywa zmian*, ed. P. Smoleń (Warsaw, 2018).

Pahl B., "Ulga inwestycyjna w podatku rolnym-problemy praktyczne", *Finanse Komunalne* No. 10 (2007).

Pahl B., "Gloss to the verdict of the Provincial Administrative Court in Gdańsk of 03.15.2006 (I SA/Gd 348/04) on land and property registration as a basis for local taxes", *Przegląd Podatków Lokalnych i Finansów Samorządowych*, No. 5 (2009).

Pietrewicz M., "Opodatkowanie działów specjalnych w indywidualnych gospodarstwach rolnych", *Finanse*, No. 12 (1975).

Pietrewicz M., *Obciążenia podatkowe rolnictwa indywidualnego i uspołecznionego* (Warsaw, 1988).

Podstawka M., "Podatek rolny od gruntów – jego ocena i potrzeba zmian", *Roczniki Naukowe* Vol. 7, part 4 (2005).

Pomorski P., "Niektóre aspekty opodatkowania rolnictwa podatkiem od nieruchomości", in: *Opodatkowanie rolnictwa w Polsce. Weryfikacja założeń, perspektywa zmian*, ed. P. Smoleń (Warsaw, 2018).

Radzikowski K., "Odrzucenie danych z ewidencji gruntów i budynków na potrzeby wymiaru podatków lokalnych w świetle najnowszego orzecznictwa sądów administracyjnych", *Samorząd Terytorialny*, No. 4 (2016).

Rocznik Statystyczny. Rolnictwo 2009, ed. M. Osiński (Warsaw, 2009).

Skorupka P., H. Anderska, Z. Łempicka (eds.), *Mały słownik języka polskiego* (Warsaw, 1968).

Sobierajewska J., "Analiza efektywności polskich gospodarstw sadowniczych na przykładzie gospodarstw z regionu Mazowsze i Podlasie", *Roczniki Naukowe Stowarzyszenia Ekonomistów Rolnictwa i Agrobiznesu*, Vol. 11, part 1 (2009).

Stanisławiszyn P., "Wykonywanie władztwa podatkowego przez gminy po nowelizacji przepisów w 2002 roku w świetle orzecznictwa regionalnych izb obrachunkowych", *Finanse Komunalne*, No. 6 (2003).

Statistical Yearbook of Agriculture, *Statistics Poland* (Warsaw, 2015).

Wierzejska J., "Motywy tworzenia podatkowych grup kapitałowych", in: *Podatkowa grupa kapitałowa*, ed. A. Nowak (Warsaw, 2015).

Wrzesińska-Nowacka A., "Podatkowa grupa kapitałowa w postępowaniu podatkowym", in: *Stanowienie i stosowanie prawa podatkowego. Procesowe prawo podatkowe*, eds. B. Kucia-Guściora, M. Munnich, A. Zdunek (Lublin, 2013).

Index

Lex et Res Publica
Polish Legal and Political Studies

Edited by
Anna Jaroń

Vol. 1 Anna Jaroń: Socio-Economic Constitutional Rights in Democratisation Processes. An Account of the Constitutional Dialogue Theory. 2012.

Vol. 2 Stanisław Filipowicz: Democracy – The Power of Illusion. 2013.

Vol. 3 Teresa Dukiet-Nagórska (ed.): The Postulates of Restorative Justice and the Continental Model of Criminal Law. As Illustrated by Polish Criminal Law. 2014.

Vol. 4 Agnieszka Kupzok: Enforcement of Patents on Geographically Divisible Inventions. An Inquiry into the Standard of Substantive Patent Law Infringement in Cross-Border Constellations. 2015.

Vol. 5 Alicja Jagielska-Burduk / Wojciech Szafrański: Legal Issues in Cultural Heritage Management. A Polish Perspective. 2016.

Vol. 6 Maciej Mataczyński (ed.): The Takeover of Public Companies as a Mode of Exercising EU Treaty Freedoms. 2017.

Vol. 7 Maciej Barczewski (ed.): Value of Information. Intellectual Property, Privacy and Big Data. 2018.

Vol. 8 Paweł Smoleń, Marcin Burzec: Introduction to Polish Tax Law. 2018.

Vol. 9 Łukasz Pohl, Konrad Burdziak: Judicial Interpretation of the 1997 Criminal Code Provisions on Self-Defence. 2019.

Vol. 10 Adam Szot: Judicial Review of Administrative Discretion. The Influence of Court Decisions on Administrative Actions. 2019.

Vol. 11 Michał Peno / Konrad Burdziak (eds.): The Concept of Modern Law. Polish and Central European Tradition. 2019.

Vol. 12 Leszek Leszczyński / Bartosz Liżewski / Adam Szot (eds.): Potential of Precedent in the Statutory Legal Order. 2019.

Vol. 13 Łukasz Bolesta: In Search of a Model for the Legal Protection of a Whistleblower in the Workplace in Poland. A legal and comparative study. 2020.

Vol. 14 Paweł Chmielnicki / Adam Sulikowski (eds.): New Perspectives on Legislation. A Comparative Approach. 2020.

Vol. 15 Marcin Burzec / Beata Kucia-Guściora / Paweł Smoleń : Agricultural Activity in Poland: A Fiscal and Legal Study. 2020.

www.peterlang.com

www.ingramcontent.com/pod-product-compliance
Ingram Content Group UK Ltd.
Pitfield, Milton Keynes, MK11 3LW, UK
UKHW021833100926
8556IPUK00004B/316

9 783631 814703